D1404656

Fabric Crafts & Other Fun

with kids

OTHER BOOKS AVAILABLE FROM CHILTON
Robbie Fanning, Series Editor

Fabric Crafts & Other Fun with kids

Projects You Can Do Together!

Susan Parker Beck
& Charlou Lunsford

Chilton Book Company
Radnor, Pennsylvania

Library of Congress Cataloging-in-Publication Data
Beck, Susan Parker.
    Fabric crafts and other fun with kids : projects you can do
together! / Susan Parker Beck, Charlou Lunsford.
        p.   cm.—(Craft kaleidoscope)
    Includes index.
    ISBN 0-8019-8616-8 (pbk.)
    1. Textile crafts.   2. Paper work.   3. Pottery craft.
I. Lunsford, Charlou.   II. Title.   III. Series.
TT699.B43   1995
745.5—dc20   94-45519
                                                            CIP

1 2 3 4 5 6 7 8 9 0   4 3 2 1 0 9 8 7 6 5

Are you interested in a quarterly newsletter about creative uses of
the sewing machine, serger, and knitting machine? Write to The
Creative Machine-s, PO Box 2634, Menlo Park, CA 94026.

To Michael
Hope you remember the fun times

—Charlou

To the child in all of us who likes to craft and create
for the sake of expression

—Susan

Contents

Foreword

I grew up in a household of laughter and sewing, but not too much craft beyond crayons. We had "art" in school, but it was of the sort where you were scolded if you did not copy the flower from the blackboard exactly. Worse, you may have crayoned outside the lines. (*The horror! The horror!*)

When you don't have a background of messing around with paint and pens, you are as disadvantaged as someone whose mother never sewed. Then you have your own child, whom you don't want to be similarly disadvantaged.

You have choices: 1) Marry a man who can wield a fierce crayon. 2) Enroll your child from birth in craft classes. 3) Read Susan Parker Beck and Charlou Lunsford's *Fabric Crafts and Other Fun with Kids*.

The ideas in here are so much fun to make for anyone of any age that I hate to see the book pigeonholed. I plan to make many of the projects as gifts. In fact, in our family, we've just rearranged the living room, moving out some chairs and moving in a 5′-long table for art activities. We know from experience that if the materials are out in the open—paper, pens, paint, glue, fabric scraps—we'll mess around with them while we're watching TV.

And there's nothing more satisfying than making things together.

Robbie Fanning
Series Editor

Acknowledgments

For their artistic talents and their smiles, many thanks go to Tristan McGrath and her mom, Kim Meinhart; Amanda and Jessica Hultgren and their mom, Jamie; Evan Meehan and his mom, Kim.

Special thanks to Michael Lunsford and all the "crafty" help he provided, Jan Dunlap and Den #10 for the Walk-on Sweatshirt, and Ben and Patricia Simmons for their excellent photography, and also to Parker Cox for his help in crafting textured paper ornaments.

Introduction

If children are around when you are working on a sewing or craft project, you usually have a helper whether you need one or not. You may be in a hurry and you definitely want your project to be perfect, but it's often worth the effort to take the time to involve your little helper in your projects or to help them do their own. Sometimes the combined efforts of an adult and a child will yield results of which you can both be proud.

This was Charlou's experience with her son. Michael was always fascinated by her sewing machine and painting projects. She soon found that it was often easier to have him "help" than to constantly say "no." Often he just wanted to feel a part of the project and very shortly his attention would go to something else of his own. Incorporating his artwork into her sewing projects, such as the pillow in Chapter 2 or the tote bag in Chapter 3, became a great way for both mother and son to have their own part in a project. Even though it takes some time and effort to plan and complete these types of projects,

the end result is a project that can be a source of pride to both mother and son.

While working with Charlou at a sewing machine store in the Kansas City area, I often saw craft and sewing projects that she and her son had made. As a child, one of my favorite activities was crafting and I loved the idea of adults working together with a child who is special to them. Together, we came up with the idea of a book full of projects that children and adults can work on together.

Along with the learning process of making a craft project, children will develop many related skills and learn all types of information as they have fun. For instance, making choices of fabrics, colors, and supplies will help strengthen thinking and decision-making skills; measuring items will expand visual and size perceptions; and following directions will aid in organizational skills.

This book is designed to provide craft and sewing projects for children of ages 3 to 12. In each project, the adult is involved in teaching and supervising the child through the steps that apply to his or her particular age. The adult will complete the item if needed so that the finished project can be enjoyed by the recipient, whether it be a child or an adult.

Many of the projects in this book are items the child will make for himself or herself: the Very Own Vest in Chapter 4, the Garment Cover and Carryall in Chapter 3, and the Woven-Flap Coin Purse in Chapter 2. Other projects are perfect gift ideas for grandparents, aunts, teachers: the Collage Planter Box in Chapter 5, the Showcase Tote in Chapter 3.

Chapter 1 discusses some of the basic understandings of the development of children. Even though each child is different, there are certain stages of skill development that can be anticipated at particular ages. Becoming familiar with these will make it easier to know at what level a child will be able to participate in the making of the projects in this book. In each chapter, after the directions for a particular project, there are guidelines for completing that project for specific age groups. This will allow you to gauge the amount of involvement needed from you as the adult directing the project.

Many of the projects detailed in Chapters 2 through 6 will work well as group activities for scouts, church youth groups, or art classes. With the additional information pertaining to the skills of particular age groups, leading a group of children through the steps needed to complete a project will be easy to organize.

Throughout the pages are places for your child's notes and ideas. Write them down to help plan projects or to remember an idea for later. This isn't school, so don't be afraid to let your child write in this book.

As you read the book and go through the projects, keep in mind that you don't necessarily need a child to begin crafting. Try a few things on your own or grab a kid and share the fun!

CHAPTER 1

Learning is Child's Play

Children, especially young children, are interested in the activities in which their parents and the adults in their lives are involved. Sewing and craft projects are fun to do and can provide the training ground for numerous practical and problem-solving skills that will benefit the child in your life for years to come. By encouraging the participation of your child, you help shape his or her identity and contribute to the building of a positive self-esteem. Working on projects together fulfills the need that children have for adult approval and gives them a feeling of worth. Making things together will create memories for both of you and provide you with useful heirlooms to treasure always.

Tips for Working with Children

When working with children, there are a few things to consider to assure that the process goes smoothly and the results are as perfect as possible. Usually, the objective of any project is to successfully complete the item started. This is even more important when children are involved so that they may feel a sense of accomplishment and learn to see things through to their conclusions. When selecting a first project to try together, choose an item or technique with which you have some familiarity. This will help initially to ensure that you will build some positive working experiences with the child. A later project might be one that could result in a learning experience for both of you as you explore the possibilities of gaining new skills for yourself as well as your child.

Even though the objective is to complete the project, the process of doing this may turn out to be completely different with children than with adults. Plan to work in short time spans as the child's interests and abilities dictate. Each child is different, however there are some general guidelines for the amount of time a child can stay focused on one activity without becoming distracted.

Use the following time limits as a starting place for noticing if the child's attention is wandering. If the child is still interested and wants to continue, then by all means allow him or her to work until the desire fades and other activities grab his or her attention.

3–4 years old	5 min.
4–5 years old	10–15 min.
6–7 years old	15–20 min.
8–9 years old	20–30 min.
10–12 yrs old	30–45 min.

Try to plan work sessions when the child is rested and in a good frame of mind so he or she will be able to concentrate as fully as possible on the task at hand.

Getting Started

Organize your projects by keeping all the needed supplies in a box or basket. This will make it easy to find everything when inspiration hits and will allow you to stop and start as needed. It also helps make cleanup a quick and easy process.

When starting a project, plan your work area and set it up to avoid as much frustration as possible. For instance, if working with paints or glue, the process will more than likely create a bit of a mess. Use aluminum foil, paper, or a vinyl tablecloth to cover the area and keep a damp cloth or paper towels handy to control spills and drips. Consider having your child wear a man's T-shirt as a smock to prevent soiling

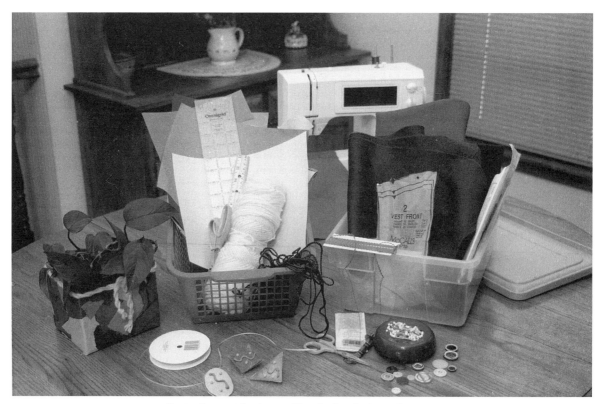

Organize project supplies in baskets or boxes.

clothing and to make cleanup easier. Think about how the child will best be able to work. It may be easier to work on the floor or standing at a table rather than sitting in a traditional work setting.

Learning Together

While wanting to maximize success, mistakes and failures will happen. Help the child to correct the mistakes if he or she asks or seems to want help. Be careful that it is something that really needs to be fixed and not just your perception of imperfection. If the child is happy with his or her work, then success has been achieved, even if it is not perfect.

Some problems may work out better if you discreetly make some corrections yourself. For instance, if working on a sewing project and stitches need to be taken out, it may be time for a break. You can remove the stitching and have the project ready for a fresh start when the child returns to it with a clear mind. Remember, there might be tears—the child's and yours—but hugs can solve a lot of problems.

When guiding children through the steps of a craft, try not to "teach" them or show them the "right way." Plan not to turn this fun activity into a schoolroom lesson. Instead of saying "We'll now learn to measure," say "Let's figure out what size we need." They not only learn how to measure, but will keep their interest in the project. Give them the general instruc-

tions and turn them loose. Don't ask or expect them to copy a project exactly. Once a child is six or older, he or she is usually able to distinguish the difference between their effort and the "perfect" model. This can cause feelings of inadequacy if their project doesn't measure up. Give them enough instruction so that they know what to do, but leave room for self-expression and creativity.

In some cases, it will be best to allow the child to decide when the project is done. For instance, when painting a shirt, two flowers may be too many for the child or twelve may not be enough. The child should be able to make this decision so that the craft item will be his or her own design. Try not to hover over the child, directing him or her toward perfection. If the glue smears or the stitching is not perfectly straight, the child will probably not be aware of this if you don't treat it as a mistake that needs to be fixed. Acceptance is a key word to remember—acceptance of the project and simultaneously of the child and his or her abilities.

Making choices is good practice in decision making. Younger children need direction and a limited number of choices; for instance, "Do you want red or blue?" will make them feel a part of the planning process, but won't overwhelm them with difficult decisions. As they get older, children are able to think more abstractly and can make complex decisions easily. Let them choose a color scheme, decide on embellishments, or finishing choices for the chosen project. Allowing children to make as many decisions about the project as possible gives them ownership and provides more motivation for completion of the project.

As you work with the child, letting him or her use "real" equipment (scissors, iron, etc.) that belongs to you shows that you respect the child enough to let him or her use things that you value. Keep in mind the child's age and ability, and make safety a priority when using sharp objects or heated items such as an iron or a glue gun.

Working on arts and crafts with your child can definitely be a learning experience for the child as well as a fun way to spend an afternoon, make a gift, or explore a new interest. But don't be surprised when you enjoy it just as much as the child and feel the same sense of accomplishment as he or she does when looking at the finished item.

Skill Levels

As you work with your child on a particular project, use the guidelines under the child's age (listed below and with each project) to help determine how much participation you and your child will share. The information listed is intended to be used as general guidelines for activities that certain age groups will be able to perform. You will know if this actually pertains to your child and you can direct him or her accordingly.

Age 3

- ✂ Can hold pencil with thumb and forefinger

- ✂ Draws crude circle with crayon
- ✂ Has some control with blunt scissors—can cut paper in two, but not along a straight line

Age 4

- ✂ Can make simple decisions between limited choices
- ✂ Will be able to paint using fingers, feet, larger brushes, and cookie cutters as stamps
- ✂ Able to handle large markers
- ✂ Can sew with an in-and-out motion using sewing cards and yarn

Ages 4–5

- ✂ Draws human stick figures or head with eyes and legs only (will add details such as hair and fingers by age 5)
- ✂ Able to fold paper
- ✂ Can cut with scissors fairly well following a straight line
- ✂ Able to manage thin markers
- ✂ Will be somewhat able to control composition and design of a collage
- ✂ Can print name if shown (age 5)
- ✂ Enjoys coloring

Age 6

- ✂ Prints name and numbers smaller and more neatly
- ✂ Threads large needle and can sew through holes in card or paper plate

✂ Can cut angular patterns such as a paper doll

Age 7

✂ Attention span is increasing and can usually carry an idea over to the next day (remembers instructions)

Age 8

✂ Can read simple directions by themselves

✂ Fine motor skills have developed well enough to use most household tools, such as a can opener and a screwdriver

✂ Pays more attention and is less distractible

Age 9

✂ Fine motor skills increase for more control of small motions

✂ Can do simple hand and machine sewing

✂ Able to learn simple knitting stitches

Ages 10–11

✂ Can make more abstract decisions (choosing fabric for a pattern)

✂ Able to plan simple designs and composition from scratch

Age 12

✂ Can usually follow easily written directions from start to finish of a project

✂ Can have enough motivation to see a project through to the end

CHAPTER 2

Machine in Motion

Teaching your child to sew is not the same as letting your child sew. Many children are fascinated by the sewing machine and its workings, but could not care less about learning to thread or clean it. This chapter is not designed to teach but to incorporate the child into your hobby. In most of the projects found in this chapter, the child

Most children are fascinated by watching the stitches form across the fabric.

simply sews and plays on the machine after you have set it up and made it ready.

A child 3 to 4 years old will be able to hold the foot control in his or her hands and press it together to make the machine run as you guide the fabric under the needle. When doing this, set your machine at a slower speed if possible and make it clear to your child that *you* say when to stop.

Children of 6 to 8 years who want to sew usually just want to see the stitches form across the fabric. Thread the machine and with some instruction on safety, let the child go. The foot control will probably need to be raised in order for a young child to be able to reach it. Place it on a stack of books tall enough to bring it to the correct height. In this middle age group, the child will need instruction on where to sew and how to change stitches, but with a bit of guidance can even program computerized stitches.

Older children who have developed an interest in sewing because of the fun they had with earlier sewing projects may show an interest in some of the more mundane aspects, such as threading. If this happens, more formal instruction on the care and set up of the machine would be appropriate. Otherwise, give the child enough instruction and supervision to do the job at hand and let it be. However, don't be surprised at how much children absorb and learn just by being exposed to something fun.

Memory Quilt

Every child can use a quilt; as a security blanket or to snuggle in while watching TV. This memory quilt can capture a year in your child's life with highlights of his or her interests and examples of artwork.

The finished size of this quilt is 39″ square, but may be made larger by adding more blocks. The squares in the quilt pictured are 13″ after seaming. The squares were cut 14″ and seamed with ½″ seam allowances. You may vary the sizes to suit your desired finished size and seam allowances. Making it from a medium-weight fabric, such as poplin, will help it to withstand lots of wear and tear.

MATERIALS

Nine squares of medium-weight fabric, each at least 14″ square. Should be a combination of solid fabrics to decorate and prints to coordinate.

1¼ yards 45″ wide single-faced quilted fabric to use as backing

4½ yards extra-wide double-fold bias binding

Thread

Scissors

Supplies needed to decorate individual squares (see below)

Sewing machine

Memory quilt.

Decorate the squares using any of the techniques described below. You may also use the techniques covered in the directions for the next project, the Cut-up Cushion. The squares may be cut larger than 14″ and trimmed to size after embellishing. Some squares may be cut from print fabrics, such as decorator fabrics used in the child's room, or from theme fabrics, such as sports, animals, or other favorites. These squares will be left unembellished.

WORD BLOCK

If you have a machine that stitches words and numbers, program words to describe important events in the life of the child, such as school, sports, scouts, pets, favorite dog, favorite foods, TV shows.

Word block.

APPLIQUÉD DRAWINGS

If you know basic appliqué techniques, it's easy to turn a simple drawing into a fabric appliqué. Choose a simple drawing the child has done and make a photocopy of it. It may be enlarged or reduced to fit onto the square. Cut out the shapes from the photocopy to use as an appliqué pattern.

Appliquéd drawing.

Arrange blocks in rows of three.

HAND AND/OR FOOT PRINTS

Decorate a square by having your child put his or her foot or hand into paint and press it onto the fabric. The child will need help with balance and placement of the print, as well as immediate help with cleaning up paint.

NAME BLOCK

Use fabric markers to have the child write his or her name on the square. On the quilt shown, the square was cut into three strips and rejoined with a strip of print fabric between the solid. You may want the child to practice on paper before writing on the fabric or you may want to trace his or her writing from the paper to the fabric.

DIRECTIONS

1. Arrange the squares in a 3 x 3 grouping.

2. Sew together with ½″ seam allowance, one row at a time. Then sew the rows together. Press seams in one direction.

3. Lay pre-quilted fabric wrong side up on a flat surface. Lay the pieced quilt top on it with the wrong side down. Pin in several places across the entire quilt to secure the top of the backing.

4. Trim back to match the top. Stitch in the ditch of the seamlines to secure the front to the backing.

5. Attach bias binding along the edges to encase the raw edges.

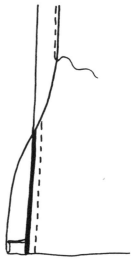

Bind edges of quilt with double-fold bias tape.

Ages 3–5

Child can:

❑ Help to select the fabrics from limited choices.

❑ Choose decorative stitches on the sewing machine that you then stitch onto the fabric.

❑ Hold the foot control to the sewing machine in his or her hands and press it together to run the machine while you guide the fabric through.

❑ Draw pictures for appliqué block.

❑ Paint block with handprints or footprints (with assistance).

❑ Write name with markers or crayons.

Ages 6–9

Child can:

❑ Help to select fabrics. Child can choose several to go with ones you have chosen.

❑ Select several decorative stitches on the machine and guide the fabrics, stitching in a random manner. Foot control may need to be raised by placing it on books for the child to be able to reach it.

❑ Program words and numbers into the machine and stitch them across the fabric. Will need some instruction in programming the machine.

❑ Draw pictures to use for appliqué design.

❑ Paint block with handprints or footprints (with assistance).

❑ Write name and words with crayons and markers.

❑ Sew the squares together. Adult can place the appropriate squares together and guide the child through the stitching process.

❑ Sit at the machine and guide the fabric to complete the seam (with supervision). Younger children may find it easier to use a ¾″ to 1″ seam allowance. If the machine has a measurement guide bar that attaches to the foot, it will be useful in helping them to sew a straight line.

❑ Help to pin the front to the backing.

Ages 10–12

Child can:

❑ Decide on color scheme and select several fabrics to use together.

❑ Choose which type of embellishments to use on particular squares.

❑ Do any of the embellishments described (may need some instruction and guidance).

❑ Sew the squares together.

❑ Pin the front to the backing.

❑ Stitch the front to the backing with instruction and supervision.

Cut-Up Cushion

Cut-up cushion.

This unusual accent pillow is just right for getting comfortable in front of the television. It's a perfect companion for the Memory Quilt pictured with it in the color section. The other pillows pictured are basic pillow shapes, one made from a co-ordinating fabric and one with a simple number appliqué fused onto the front.

Coordinating pillows.

When working on craft and sewing projects, children learn more than the techniques needed to complete the item. While stitching this cushion, a child will learn how to make decisions by selecting fabrics, colors, stitches, and threads. He or she will also experience making creative choices when designing the front of the pillow and deciding how it will all go together.

MATERIALS

Five to six large swatches of various fabrics (these will be trimmed to needed sizes at a later time)

20″ square of fabric for backing

Polyester stuffing material

Sewing machine

Iron

Thread

Scissors

Pull-away type of stabilizer or lightweight typing paper

Other supplies as needed for decorating swatches (decorative threads, cords, etc.—see directions below)

Decorate swatches of fabric using any of the techniques described below.

RANDOM MACHINE STITCHING

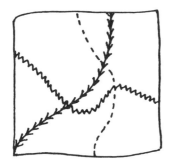

Random machine stitching.

Select one or more stitches on the machine and stitch across a swatch of fabric in any manner desired. You will need to put stabilizer or paper behind the fabric to keep it from pulling or puckering. Pull away after stitching is complete.

PATTERN STITCHING

Stitching in a specific pattern.

Similar to random stitching, except that you follow a specific pattern that has been marked on the fabric as a stitching guide.

WORDS AND NUMBERS

Using a computerized sewing machine equipped with preprogrammed letters and numbers, select your name, a slogan, or any other words you want and stitch, following the directions for that particular machine.

DESIGNER STITCHES

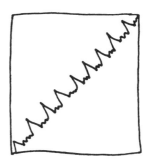

Design your own decorative stitches.

If your sewing machine is equipped with a design feature, make up your own pattern of stitches. Again, follow manufacturer's directions.

COUCHING

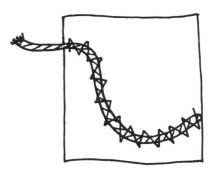

Couch a cord onto the surface of the fabric.

Similar to decorative stitching, however, this time you will do your stitching over a length of yarn or decorative cord. Place the cord under the presser foot and stitch as before. Check to see if your machine has available a special foot designed to hold the yarn or cord.

15

PRINT SWATCH

Choose a coordinating colorful swatch of print fabric that needs no further embellishment.

DIRECTIONS

1. Trim swatches to be squares or rectangles of different random sizes.

2. Arrange swatches in a pleasing arrangement to form a 19″ square. Lay them out on a floor or tabletop and stand back to take a look. Rearrange several times to see the possibilities of design.

Arrange swatches in a 19″ square.

3. Stitch trimmed squares and rectangles together to form an approximate 19″ square. Trim swatches as needed to fit together easily.

4. Cut backing fabric to be the same size as the pieced front.

5. Place front and back right sides together. Stitch around all sides, about ½″ to ¾″ from all edges, leaving a 6″ to 8″ opening on one side.

Stitch around sides to form a pocket for stuffing.

6. Trim fabric at the corners at a diagonal, being careful not to cut through the stitching.

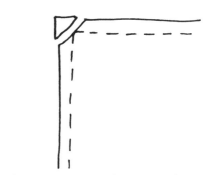

Trim corners at a diagonal before turning.

7. Turn right side out. Press.

8. Stuff with polyester stuffing until the cushion is as full as you would like.

9. Close the opening by folding the edges in and machine stitching together.

NOTE: If an adult is sewing the pillow, he or she may want to add finishing details, such as piping, ruffles, or a zippered opening for a pillow form. The pillow shown in the color section has piped edges.

Ages 3–5

Child can:

❑ Help to select the fabrics. Give the child a choice of two to three fabrics. Have him or her choose one to complement others that you have chosen.

❑ Choose one or more decorative stitches on the sewing machine that you will then stitch onto the swatches.

❑ Hold the foot control to the sewing machine in his or her hands and press together to run the machine while you guide the fabric through.

❑ Assist in stuffing the cushion with fiberfill.

Ages 6–9

Child can:

❑ Help to select fabrics. Start with a print that you have selected (possibly a remnant of fabrics used in the child's room). Let him or her choose three to four other fabrics to go with the print.

❑ Select several decorative stitches and guide the fabric through the machine to stitch on the swatch in a random manner. The foot control may need to be raised by placing it on books for the child to be able to reach it.

❑ Program his or her name or design original stitch patterns using a computerized sewing machine, depending on the capabilities of the machine. An adult should lead the child through the programming steps and supervise the stitching.

❑ Assist in arranging patches to form a 19″ square. Lay them out on a table and help the child to see how they can fit together to form a square. Keep the swatches fairly large and the design simple.

❑ Help to sew swatches together to complete the front of the cushion.

❑ After the front is designed, an adult can place the appropriate swatches together and start the seam. A supervised child can sit at the machine and guide the fabric to complete the seam. Younger children may find it easier to use a ³⁄₄″ to 1″ seam allowance. If the machine has a measurement guide bar that attaches to the foot, it will be useful in helping them to sew a straight line.

❑ Turn the pillow right side out and stuff until full. An adult will sew the opening closed to finish.

Ages 10–12

Child can:

❑ Decide on color scheme and select several fabrics to use together.

❑ Choose decorative stitches on the sewing machine and stitch them onto fabric following a specific pattern.

❑ Program name, words, sentences, and design a more complex stitch pattern on a computerized machine.

❑ Couch cords onto fabric by stitching over decorative cords or yarns using a special presser for the machine, if available.

❑ Trim swatches and design the front of the cushion.

❑ Trim backing fabric to be the same size as the front of the pillow.

❑ Stitch the front and back of the pillow together with instruction and supervision.

❑ Turn the pillow right side out, press, and stuff with fiberfill.

❑ Sew opening closed with adult instruction and supervision.

NOTE: Depending on skill level and experience, a child in this age group may be able to complete most of this project with minimal supervision.

Ribbon Riot

Leftover pieces of ribbons and buttons combined with decorative stitches from the sewing machine will make fun personalized badges or bookmarkers. These are great gift ideas for friends, teachers, and just about anyone who enjoys a good book now and then.

The ribbons will be easier to handle and decorate with stitches if they are stabilized and stiffened in some way. There are two types of stabilizers on the market that are easy to use and work well for the ribbons. One is a brush-on liquid called Perfect Sew. Using a brush or your fingers, saturate the ribbon and let dry before stitching. Another product, called Lite Fabric Stiffener, is an aerosol that is lightly sprayed onto the ribbon to stiffen it. Both products will make the ribbon stiff, similar to paper, making it easy to stitch through.

NOTE: It is recommended to keep aerosols away from children because of their flammability. They should be used by an adult.

To speed drying, use a hair dryer at a low temperature or press with a warm iron. After stitching, wash the ribbons to remove the stabilizer. Lightly press to set the stitches and flatten the ribbon.

Award Badges

Use these cute ribbon badges as rewards for good behavior, passed tests, or just to say "You're a great kid!"

Award badge.

Badge #1

MATERIALS

1½" button to cover

Scrap of fabric large enough to cover button

10" of ⅝" ribbon

10" of ⅜" ribbon

Stabilizer

Purchased star appliqué patch

Contrasting or metallic thread

Sewing machine

Seam sealant

Pin back

Fabric glue

DIRECTIONS

1. Cover the button with fabric and glue the star appliqué in center.

2. Stabilize ribbons with liquid or spray stabilizer. Let dry.

3. Using metallic or contrasting thread, zigzag (width 1½", length 1½") along both edges of the wider ribbon.

4. Stitch down the center of the narrow ribbon using a decorative stitch of your choice.

5. Fold the wider ribbon at the midpoint to form a triangle. Stitch or glue to secure. Fold narrow ribbon the same way and secure.

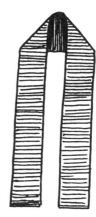

Fold ribbon to form mitered point.

6. Place the narrow ribbon on top of the wider ribbon. Stitch or glue together.

7. Hand sew or glue the folded edge (top) of the ribbon to the shank on back of the button.

8. Glue or stitch the pin back to the back of the button.

9. Trim lower edges of ribbons to shape desired. Apply seam sealant to trimmed edges. Let dry.

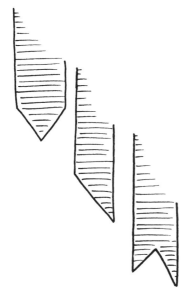

Trim ends of ribbon to desired shape.

Badge #2

MATERIALS

6″ of 1½″ ribbon

6″ of ⅝″ ribbon

1¾″ purchased star appliqué patch

Stabilizer

Metallic thread

Pin back

Sewing machine

DIRECTIONS

1. Stabilize ribbons with liquid or spray stabilizer. Let dry.

2. Stitch the narrow ribbon with your choice of decorative stitch or, if your sewing machine will stitch letters, choose an appropriate saying, such as Number 1 Kid, Star of the Week, Birthday Boy, Super Star, etc.

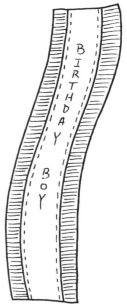

Stitch appropriate message on narrow ribbon before edgestitching it onto wider ribbon.

3. Center the narrow ribbon on top of the wider ribbon and edgestitch in place.

4. Turn the top edge under ¼″ and stitch to the hem.

5. Sew the star appliqué to the top hemmed edge.

6. Glue or stitch the pin back to the back of the appliqué patch.

7. Trim lower edges of the ribbon to desired shape. Seal cut edges with seam sealant. Let dry.

Design your own Badge here:

Bookmarkers

Bookmarkers are practical items that can be personalized with the reader's name or special interests.

Marker #1

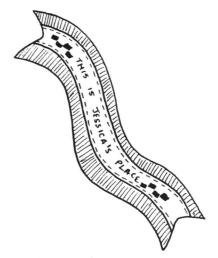

Personalized bookmark.

MATERIALS

12″ of 1½″ ribbon

12″ of ⅝″ ribbon

Stabilizer

Seam sealant

Contrasting thread

Sewing machine

DIRECTIONS

1. Stabilize the ribbons with liquid or spray stabilizer. Let dry.

2. With decorative stitches or programmed words, stitch down the center of the narrow ribbon. (Examples of words—"This is Jessica's place" or "Don't lose this place.")

3. Center the narrow ribbon on top of the wider ribbon and edgestitch in place.

4. Trim edges and seal cut edges with seam sealant. Let dry.

Books I want to read:

_____

_____

_____

_____

_____

_____

_____

_____

_____

_____

_____

_____

_____

_____

Marker #2

Basketball bookmark.

MATERIALS

20″ of ⅜″ ribbon

Two shank buttons

Stabilizer

Contrasting thread

Sewing machine

DIRECTIONS

1. Stabilize ribbon with liquid or spray stabilizer. Let dry.

2. Stitch decorative stitches or words down the center of the ribbon as desired.

3. Thread each end of ribbon through the shank of one of the buttons. Tie the end of the ribbon in a knot below the button.

NOTE: If the button is large enough to slide around on the ribbon, tie a second knot above the button to hold it in place at the end of the ribbon.

Marker #3

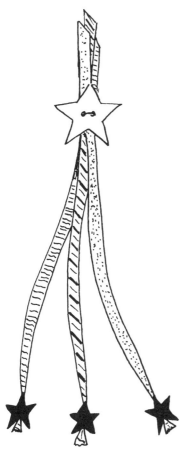

Triple ribbon marker.

MATERIALS

Three 15″ pieces of ³⁄₈″ ribbon

Buttons, charms, or beads

Stabilizer

Contrasting thread

Sewing machine

DIRECTIONS

1. Thread one end of each ribbon through the button, bead, or charm. Tie a knot or stitch the ribbon together to secure.

2. Secure the unfinished ends in one of the following ways: (a) Layer the three ribbons on top of each other. Place a button or purchased appliqué patch on top of the ribbon ends and stitch in place; (b) Layer ribbons on top of each other and slip through a ring. Fold over and stitch ends down. Add charms to ring if desired; (c) Layer ribbons and make three loops at the top. Stitch together. Sew a button or charm over stitching if desired.

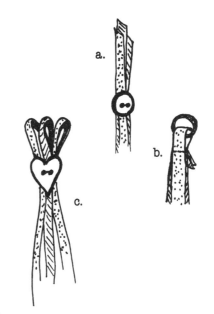

Options for finishing the top of the bookmark.

Ages 3–5

Child can:

- ❏ Select color of ribbon for badge or marker.
- ❏ Help to paint stabilizer on ribbon.
- ❏ Choose decorative stitches for sewing on the ribbon.
- ❏ Select buttons or charms for markers.

Ages 6–9

Child can:

- ❏ Choose color of ribbon for badge or marker.
- ❏ Paint stabilizer on ribbon and use a hair dryer or iron (with supervision) to speed drying.
- ❏ Select decorative stitches or sayings to be stitched on ribbon.
- ❏ Program letters and words into sewing machine for stitching.
- ❏ Guide ribbon under the needle to sew letters or stitches.
- ❏ Attach buttons and/or charms to end of ribbons.
- ❏ Apply seam sealant to cut edges.

Ages 10–12

Child can:

- ❏ Complete all steps for making badges and markers. May need some instruction and supervision using the sewing machine.

Woven-Flap Coin Purses

The body of these small purses are made from scraps of fabric with the closure flap woven from strips of coordinating fabrics.

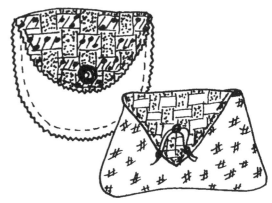

Woven-flap coin purses.

Firmly woven fabric for the body of the purse. Felt or wool works well, however medium-weight cotton interfaced with a fusible interfacing will also be heavy enough (Half-Circle Purse requires a 16″ x 8″ piece. Triangular Purse requires a 12″ x 8″ piece.)

Two contrasting pieces of light- to medium-weight fabric for weaving the flap. You will need a pinnable surface such as an ironing board or cutting surface for weaving. (To make woven fabric flaps for both coin purses, you will need enough fabric to cut or tear into thirty strips, each ½″ x 6″.)

Fusible interfacing (15″ x 6″)

Button or tie for closure

Thread

Sewing machine

Steam iron

Velcro closures

Pinking shears (optional)

Half-Circle Purse

DIRECTIONS

1. Cut or tear contrasting fabrics into ½″ x 6″ strips.

2. To weave the flap of the purse, arrange the strips of one fabric side by side. Place a pin in each end to hold in place.

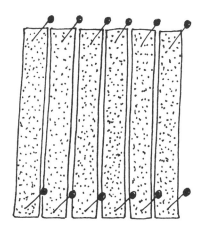

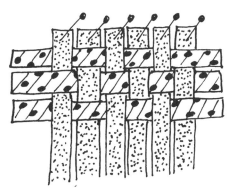

Simple over and under weaving.

3. Combine the two fabrics by weaving the contrasting fabric strips over and under the strips pinned in place. Position the strips closely together to form a solid piece of fabric.

4. Carefully unpin the strips and turn the woven fabric over with wrong side up. Using the steam iron,

25

fuse interfacing to the wrong side of the woven fabric to form backing.

5. Using pattern piece A from the pattern section, cut a flap from the woven piece of fabric, using pinking shears if desired.

6. Cut two pieces for the body of the purse from pattern piece B. Use pinking shears if desired.

7. Place the flap and one of the body pieces right sides together, matching the straight edges. Using a ¼″ seam allowance, sew the flap to the purse. Open out the seam and edgestitch on the right side of the flap a scant ¼″ from the seamline. Continue edgestitching along the cut edges of the flap.

10. Sew other side of the Velcro closure to the wrong side of the flap, matching position with the Velcro on the body.

11. Stitch a decorative button on right side of the flap, positioning it over the Velcro closure.

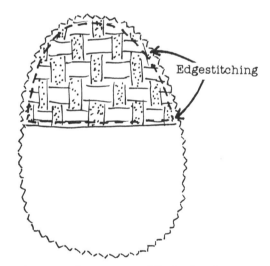

Sew the flap to one of the body pieces.

8. Stitch the Velcro closure on the right side at the center of the straight edge on the remaining body piece, centered from side to side.

9. Place the two pieces of the body wrong sides together and stitch a scant ¼″ from the edge.

ID CARD

Name _____

Address _____

_____

Phone _____

Triangular Purse

DIRECTIONS

1. Weave fabric for flap following steps 1 through 4 in the Half-Circle Purse directions.

2. Cut the flap from the woven fabric using pattern piece A from the pattern section.

3. Cut one piece for the body of the purse using pattern piece B from the pattern section.

4. Place the flap and the body piece right sides together, lining up the straight edges. Stitch together straight edges, using a ¼" seam allowance. Open out the seam allowance and topstitch a scant ¼" on each side of the seamline.

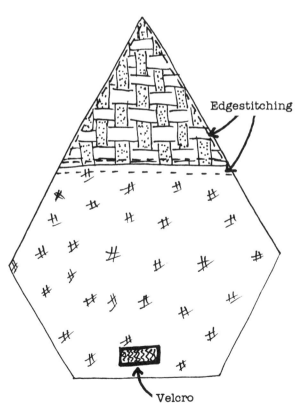

Attach the flap and Velcro closure to one of the body pieces.

5. Stitch the Velcro closure ½" from the cut front edge of body, centered from side to side.

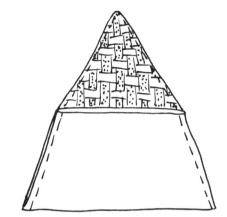

Fold the purse right sides together and stitch.

6. Fold the body of the purse wrong sides together and stitch sides a scant ¼" from the edges.

7. Stitch the other side of the Velcro closure on the wrong side of the flap, matching the position with the Velcro on the body.

8. Make a decorative closure by cutting a strip of fabric ¾" x 5". Fold it right sides together and stitch along the 5" side using a ¼" seam allowance. Trim the seam, turn, and press. Tie into a knot, adding beads if desired. Sew the closure onto front of flap, positioning it over the Velcro closure.

Ages 3–5

Child can:

❑ Help to select fabrics used from a limited selection.

❑ Help to slide across strips into place after an adult has woven it through the vertical strips.

❑ Select button to use as closure.

27

Ages 6–9

Child can:

- ❑ Select fabrics to be used.
- ❑ Cut or tear strips for weaving.
- ❑ Pin strips into place for weaving.
- ❑ Weave cross strips over and under with some instruction.
- ❑ Cut out body of purse and flap after interfacing has been fused.
- ❑ Place pieces together and sew with some instruction.
- ❑ Attach decorative button or tie closure.

Ages 10–12

Child can:

- ❑ Select fabrics to be used.
- ❑ Cut or tear strips for weaving.
- ❑ Pin strips into place for weaving.
- ❑ Weave cross strips over and under with some instruction.
- ❑ Help to fuse interfacing to back of woven strips.
- ❑ Cut out body and flap of purse.
- ❑ Place pieces together and sew with some instruction.
- ❑ Stitch Velcro closure in place.
- ❑ Attach decorative button or tie closure.

NOTES

_____

_____

_____

_____

_____

_____

_____

_____

_____

_____

_____

CHAPTER 3

Splashes of Color

Crayons and Markers

One of the earliest structured learning activities in which a child is involved is coloring with crayons and markers. The bright colors and freedom of design unleashes the artist in all of us as we learn to handle drawing and writing implements. Children love to draw and color pictures of things and people that are familiar to them. It's an easy transition from drawing on paper to drawing on fabric and you can put this original artwork to good use by turning it into practical articles such as notebook covers and tote bags.

When working with fabric crayons, be aware that there are two different types available. For best results, check the specific instructions that come with the type you choose.

The first type allows you to draw directly onto the fabric. Available in a variety of colors, the colors become permanent after heat setting with an iron according to the instructions.

The second type of fabric crayons requires two steps. The design first is drawn onto paper and then is transferred to the fabric with an iron. The advantage to using this type is that the child may draw several designs or pictures on paper and you can choose the one that will work best for the item you plan to make. It also allows you to control the placement of the picture on the fabric. This works well for younger children who may need to practice a bit before producing a work of art.

Because the designs transfer in reverse, any printing or writing (the name of the child, the date of the proj-

Reverse writing for transferring onto fabric.

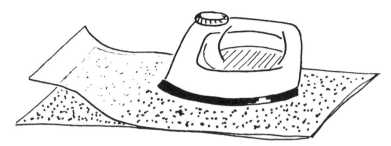

Applying laminating vinyl to fabric.

ect) must be written in mirror image. Have the child write on paper and you can then transfer it in reverse to another piece to be ironed onto the fabric. To do this, use a light box or a window on a sunny day. Tape the original to the window with the letters facing outside. You will see the reverse as the sun shines through. Tape another piece of paper over it and trace the backwards letters with the same colors. When the reversed letters are ironed onto the fabric, they will be readable as the child wrote them. When transferring the picture to fabric, follow the instructions provided with the crayons. This should usually be done by an adult, although some older children will be able to handle the iron with some close supervision.

Fabric markers are available as an alternative to crayons. The markers are permanent and are designed to be used directly on the fabric. They come in all styles: thin, wide, pointed, rounded, and chisel tips. Some must be pressed with a warm iron to set the colors. The markers may bleed through the fabric so have the child work with the fabric on cardboard or several layers of paper to protect the work surface.

Preserving Your Project

Laminating is a great way to make the project durable and easy to clean, especially since the fabric will probably be white or a light color in order to make the colors show up. There are iron-on laminating products now available to the home crafter. The products are easily applied with a dry iron following the specific instructions that come with it. It is usually best to laminate an area larger than needed and then cut to finished size.

Use pins on the laminated fabric in the seam allowance only, as they will leave small holes. Better yet, use tape or hair clips to hold pieces together. Use a slightly longer than normal stitch length of 6 to 8 stitches per inch. Finger press the seams as you sew. Laminating is easy to do and gives a finished, store-bought look to your child's artwork that is made into practical objects.

Collector Cover

Collector cover.

A tabletop or floor area allows enough room for measuring and drawing.

Your child can make a personalized notebook for his or her trading card collection. While the traditional baseball cards are still popular, cards are also available for cartoon characters and favorite TV shows. If the child is not a card collector, the notebook can be used as a photo album, journal, or scrapbook. The inside of the notebook can hold any type of paper, plastic pockets, or holders needed for the purpose selected.

Along with encouraging artistic expression and creativity, this project will help develop measuring skills and size perceptions. A tabletop or floor area will be needed to allow enough room for measuring and drawing.

MATERIALS

Three-ring binder

½ yard fabric for cover—medium-weight, firmly woven, light colors work best with crayons and markers

½ yard of laminating vinyl

Yardstick or tape measure

Vanishing or water-soluble fabric marker

Scissors

Thread in a color to match fabric

Sewing machine

Iron

31

Measuring helps to strengthen visual perception skills.

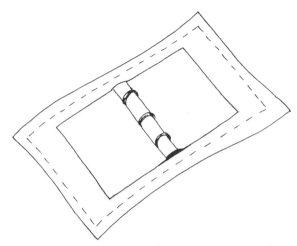

Mark fabric by adding 4″ to each end and 1″ to top and bottom edges.

ate allowances (e.g., 11½″ + 1″ + 1″ = 13½″ and 22″ + 4″ + 4″ = 30″).

Visually—Lay the binder out flat and place a tape measure along the edge. Have the child reposition the tape so that 4″ extends beyond the edge of the binder. Repeat along the sides with 1″ extending past the top and bottom of the binder. This will reinforce the idea of adding allowances around all four edges.

2. To determine areas for drawing, measure the front, spine, and back of the binder. For picture placement, further divide the fabric into front,

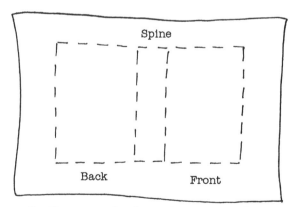

Outline areas for front, back, and spine.

DIRECTIONS

1. Open the binder so that it lies flat on the fabric. Measure the fabric by adding 1″ to the top and bottom edges of the binder. Add 4″ on each end to allow for flaps. Using a fabric marker, draw the rectangle on the fabric. Trim away most of the excess fabric, leaving about 2″ around the drawn rectangle.

TIPS: Help your child measure the fabric using one of the following ways:

Mathematically—Measure the notebook and have your child figure the needed fabric by adding the appropri-

spine, and back sections, keeping in mind that the front will be the right half of the cover.

3. Draw and color designs and pictures with fabric markers. If there is to be a title for the book, remember to place it along the spine.

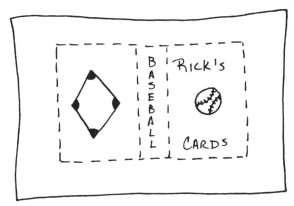

Draw and color designs and pictures with fabric markers.

4. Laminate the embellished fabric before cutting it to the drawn size. The extra border will make it easier to handle and keep the edges from unraveling as you work with it.

5. Fold 3¾" in on each side with right sides together (the extra ¼" is allowed for ease). Stitch across the top and bottom using a ¾" seam allowance. Turn right side out (trim corners at a diagonal if needed in order to form a sharp corner).

6. Finger press (to the inside) the seam allowance (¾") along the center of the top and bottom of the cover. There is no need to finish the edges as the laminate will keep them from wearing.

7. Insert the notebook into the cover by placing the binder into the side flaps. You may need to open the cover backwards to insert the binder into the second flap.

Ages 3–5

Child can:

❏ Select fabric from a limited selection of two or three choices.

❏ Choose crayons or markers with which to draw—child may have a preference.

❏ Draw pictures and color in the area designated.

Ages 6–9

Child can:

❏ Select fabrics and markers or crayons.

❏ Help to measure the notebook with yardstick or tape measure and understand the concept of adding to all sides for allowance.

❏ Help to define the areas in which to draw and write.

❏ Draw and write desired designs on the marked fabric.

❏ Cut out the embellished notebook cover.

❏ Sew flaps in place with some instruction and supervision regarding the sewing machine.

Ages 10–12

Child can:

❏ Select fabric and markers or crayons.

❏ Measure the binder and determine the needed size for the cover.

❏ Help to define the areas in which to draw and write.

❏ Draw and write desired designs on the marked fabric.

❏ Help with the laminating process of the embellished fabric.

❏ Cut out the notebook cover.

❏ Sew the flaps in place with some instruction and supervision regarding the sewing machine.

I need a notebook to collect:

_____

_____

_____

_____

_____

_____

_____

_____

_____

_____

_____

_____

_____

_____

Showcase Tote

Showcase tote.

A tote bag is not only functional, but it's also a great way to display your child's artwork. This is a great gift idea for grandma or a favorite aunt. Along with the artist's name or signature, be sure to include a date or the child's age on this keepsake.

MATERIALS

$5/8$ yard medium-weight fabric (White or light colors will allow the drawings to show the best. You may want to allow extra fabric for mistakes in drawing.)

$1/2$ yard medium-weight fabric for lining (lightweight vinyl or shower curtain is a good choice if the bag will be used for damp items)

Fabric markers

Scissors

Iron

Sewing machine

Interfacing—two pieces, 16″ x 18″ (for extra stability use extra-firm craft type of interfacing)

Thread to match fabric

⅝ yard laminating vinyl

6. To make the flat base at the bottom of the bag, fold so that the bottom seam lines up with the side seam, forming a point at the corner. Measure down 2¼″ from the point

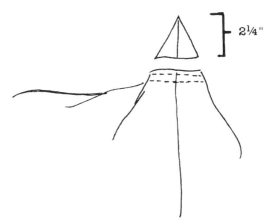

Stitching corners to form a flat base.

DIRECTIONS

1. Using a fabric marker, outline the following pieces on the fabric. Do not cut out at this time.

Front and back—two rectangles, 16″ x 18″

Top band—4″ x 35″

Handles—two strips, 3¼″ x 20″

2. Draw and color designs and pictures on the outlined front and back pieces of the tote bag. You can also color the band and the handles if desired.

3. Cut out pieces, leaving a 1″ to 2″ border on all sides of all pieces. Laminate the pieces that make up the tote bag, including the band and the handles.

4. Trim excess fabric away from the edges of the drawn pieces. Baste interfacing to the wrong sides of the front and the back of the tote bag.

5. With right sides together, stitch the sides and the bottom of the bag with a ½″ seam allowance. Repeat with lining pieces.

and stitch across the bottom to form a triangle. Stitch again ¼″ from the first stitching and cut off the point near this second stitching. Repeat with the lining.

7. Turn the bag only right side out. Put the lining inside the bag with wrong sides together, matching side seams. Baste the raw edges together.

8. Sew the band with right sides together along the 4″ side to form a circle. Use a ½″ seam allowance and press the seam open after stitching.

9. Place the band along the top raw edge of the bag with right sides together. Stitch along the raw edges through the band, bag, and lining, using a ½″ seam allowance. Finger press seam allowance up toward the band.

Stitch band to top edge of tote with right sides together.

10. Fold the band with 2″ to the inside of the bag. Edgestitch the band on the outside of the bag, catching the edge on the inside as you sew.

11. To make handles, fold ¼″ under on one long side. Finger press. Fold the strip into thirds with the raw edge to the inside. Edgestitch down both long edges.

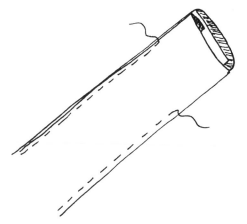

Edgestitch long sides of handles.

12. To attach handles, measure 5″ in from the side seam and 1½″ down

from the top edge. Fold under ½″ on the end of the handle and position at the measured place. Stitch in place using an hourglass pattern for strength.

Stitch handles to bag using hourglass pattern.

Ages 3–5

Child can:

- ❑ Help mark areas to be cut out.
- ❑ Draw with crayons on paper. May need to give the child some ideas of what to draw. Adult will transfer design to fabric.

Ages 6–9

Child can:

- ❑ Select crayons or markers to use.
- ❑ Draw and color on paper or fabric.
- ❑ Help measure and mark areas to be cut out.

❑ Cut out the tote bag with some direction and supervision.

❑ Stitch straight sides of the tote with some direction and supervision.

Ages 10–12

Child can:

❑ Design and create a picture around a theme (e.g., a beach bag, or to coordinate with a particular print fabric).

❑ Mark and cut out the tote bag.

❑ Sew tote bag together with some direction and supervision (may need help sewing the band and/or handles).

NOTE: With all age groups, laminating should be done by an adult. (Older children may be able to do this if closely supervised by an adult.)

Painting Techniques

Every child loves to paint! Remember finger painting and how much fun it was to really let yourself go? Today's kids have so many choices of colors, techniques, and tools that it opens up a whole new world of creativity. Advancing from crayons and markers moves the young artist to paints and brushes. The simplest type of painting to learn is fabric painting, not only with brushes, fingers, and toes, but also with unusual items found around the house.

Today's budding young artists.

The paints on the market today include dozens of brands and types; shiny and glittery, dimensional or flat, pearls and neons. Most manufacturers have brochures and booklets available about their brands of paint. For best results, heed their recommendations and pay attention to the following general guidelines.

In most cases, a natural fiber or a natural-fiber blend will work best as a surface for the paints. Pre-wash and dry the garment or fabric without using fabric softener. This will remove any sizing and allow the paint to adhere well to the surface. If necessary, press to remove wrinkles.

Cover the work area before beginning a project. Large plastic trash bags work well for this, as does aluminum foil, waxed paper, or a vinyl tablecloth. Be prepared for this to be a messy procedure—that's part of the appeal to the kids! Setting up near a sink area and keeping damp paper towels ready is a good idea. Each child should wear a paint shirt or smock with rolled-up sleeves. A large adult T-shirt is an easy, inexpensive way to control the cleanup of the child.

Start a project in the area furthest away and work toward you. This will help avoid dragging sleeves and arms across the wet portions. Let the paint dry 20 to 30 minutes (if the children can wait!) before adding another color to a specific area. Shake the paint down into the tip of the bottle before starting. Practice on a scrap or on a paper towel to get used to the way the

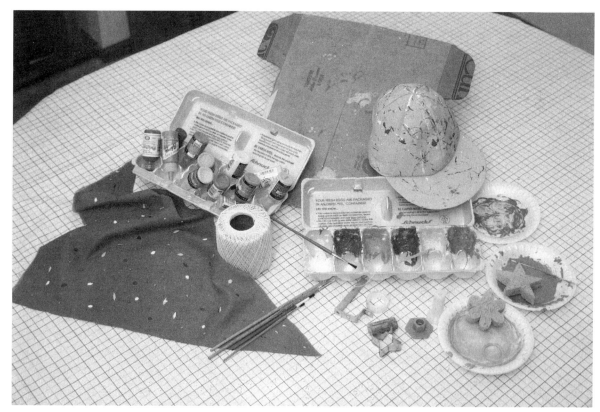

Use egg cartons and paper plates to keep paints ready to go.

paint flows. Keep the tip clean by wiping it periodically with a paper towel. Turn the paint bottle upside down in an empty egg carton when not in use. This will keep it ready to go with the paint in the tip.

Let the painted item dry 12 to 24 hours before wearing and at least 72 hours before washing. To wash, turn the garment inside out and machine wash on the gentle cycle. Use warm water and fabric softener, which helps to keep the paint soft. Air dry.

If a garment needs pressing, do not touch the iron to the paint. Turn it inside out with a terry-cloth towel under the painted area. Steam or press lightly from the wrong side.

When the urge to paint strikes, don't run out to buy a new item to paint. An old T-shirt with a small stain is a candidate for being painted. An adult T-shirt makes a great sleep shirt. Especially if you have some glow-in-the dark paint.

Don't worry about being creative; dots, squiggles and random lines will please young children. Older kids will have their own ideas. For example, a design from their favorite super hero's uniform or their school mascot. On the frilly or more feminine side, add trims, buttons, bows and laces to your design.

Painting with kids can be fun. Letting them do their own project may give you time to finish yours, so everyone can create their own masterpiece.

Splattered Accessories

If you've ever had to help with a field trip or day camp, you know how quickly one child looks like another in a group. The kids under your care would be much easier to spot if they all had matching hats or neckerchiefs to distinguish them from the crowds. These items can be simple to make and the children will enjoy wearing them, especially if they have had a hand in designing them.

The items painted can be ready-made or hand-sewn. Blank hats, vests, and scarves can be found at most craft stores in various sizes. Neckerchiefs are easily made from a triangular piece of fabric. To make four, use ⅔ yard of 45″ wide broadcloth or lightweight cotton and cut as shown. Edges may be hemmed, pinked, fringed, or serged.

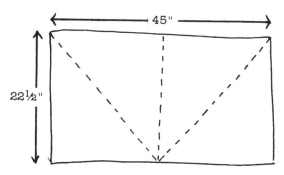

Cut four neckerchiefs from ⅔ yard of fabric.

To splatter paint accessories, follow these easy steps.

MATERIALS

Accessory item to be painted (shoes, cap, neckerchief)

Various colors of fabric paint

Shallow box lined with waxed paper, large enough to hold item

DIRECTIONS

1. Protect your work area, otherwise the accessories may not be the only things splattered. Place small items, such as shoes or a cap, in a shallow box lined with waxed paper to help contain the splatters.

2. Stuff hats and shoes lightly with paper and leave stuffed until the paint is dry. Put garments over cardboard; a purchased shirt board or cardboard covered with waxed paper will keep the paint from soaking through to the other side. If you are painting both sides of a garment, let the first side dry before turning it over to paint the other side.

3. There are two easy ways to get a splattered look to your painting. Try each of these to get different effects with your paint: (a) Squeeze the paint right from the tube to make dots or squiggles. The tip does not need to touch the project, and to vary the splatter hold the paint above and let it drip onto the item; (b) Cut string into 12" to 18" lengths. Saturate the string by dipping it into paint poured into a shallow dish or an egg carton. Leave about 4" to 6" of the string out of the paint in order to have a clean handle. If needed, use a paintbrush to push the string down into the paint to be

sure it's well covered. Lay the string on the item and tap in place or drag across for a streaked effect.

Ages 3–5

Child can:

❑ Choose the color of the item to be painted.

❑ Choose the color(s) of paint to be used.

❑ Help to stuff the shoes or cap with paper.

❑ Squeeze drops of paint onto the item.

❑ Place the string into the paint and onto the item with the help of an adult.

Ages 6–9

Child can:

❑ Choose the color of the item to be painted.

❑ Choose the color(s) of paint to be used.

❑ Stuff the shoes or cap with paper.

❑ Squeeze drops of paint onto the item.

❑ Place the string into the paint and onto the item with instruction.

Ages 10–12

Child can:

❑ Choose the color of the item to be painted.

❑ Choose the color(s) of paint to be used.

- ❑ Prepare a box with waxed paper lining.

- ❑ Stuff the shoes or cap with paper.

- ❑ Squeeze drops of paint onto the item.

- ❑ Place the string into the paint and onto the item with instruction.

- ❑ Combine painting techniques for a more complex design.

My favorite paint colors:

_____

_____

_____

_____

_____

_____

_____

_____

_____

_____

_____

_____

_____

_____

Sponge-Painted T-Shirt

Sponge-painted shirt.

The T-shirts shown in the color section were sponge-painted by a five-year-old who had a great time designing her own look. Sponge painting is an easy and fun way for even the youngest child to participate in crafting. It is simple and fits with a limited attention span. This technique can be used on almost any item that can be laid out flat in order to press the paint-filled sponge onto it.

Sponges may be purchased precut into shapes or you may cut your own shapes to use. Any simple shape will work: geometrics, flowers, stars, moon, and so on. Cookie cutters are great to use as patterns for cutting the sponge. Look for sponges with different textures, as they will give different surface looks to the paint. Use a damp sponge and dip it into a shallow amount of paint. Be careful not to have the sponge too wet or the paint will likely bleed into the fabric, blurring the edges of the shape. With cardboard and waxed paper behind the project, place the paint-filled

41

Sponge shapes are used to create a one-of-a-kind T-shirt.

sponge on the surface and press to release the paint. The harder and longer you press, the more solid the shape will be painted onto the surface. Don't be concerned if the paint smears or drips a bit—it can add to the overall design.

After sponge painting the shapes onto the surface of the project, finish the design by adding accents of paint in coordinating or contrasting colors. Glitter and neons could also be used to accentuate the basic design.

MATERIALS

Purchased or sewn T-shirt, pre-washed without fabric softener

Desired colors of fabric paint

Sponges cut into desired shapes

Purchased shirtboard or cardboard covered with waxed paper

DIRECTIONS

1. Place the T-shirt over the cardboard.

2. Put a small amount of paint into a shallow dish. Dip a sponge shape into paint, covering one side.

3. Press the sponge onto the front of the T-shirt where desired. Continue until the design is as you want it.

4. After the sponge design is dry, apply additional embellishments, such as outlining, dots, and squiggles.

Ages 3–5

Child can:

❑ Choose the color of the shirt to be painted, from a limited selection.

❑ Select the color(s) of paint to be used.

❑ Help to squeeze paint into a shallow dish.

❑ Place the sponge in paint with some supervision.

❑ Press the paint-filled sponge onto the shirt.

Ages 6–9

Child can:

❑ Choose the color of the shirt to be painted.

❑ Select the color(s) of paint to be used.

❑ Squeeze paint into a shallow dish.

❑ Place the sponge in paint.

❑ Press the paint-filled sponge onto the shirt.

❑ Outline simple shapes after drying.

❑ Add simple finishing embellishments.

Ages 10–12

Child can:

❑ Choose the color of the shirt to be painted.

❑ Select the color(s) of paint to be used.

❑ Squeeze paint into a shallow dish.

❑ Place the sponge in paint.

❑ Press the sponges onto the shirt, creating more complex designs.

❑ Outline shapes after drying.

❑ Add more elaborate finishing embellishments.

Designing my T-shirt:

T-shirt color:

_____

Sponge shapes:

_____

_____

_____

Paint colors:

_____

_____

_____

Garment Cover and Carryall

Garment cover and carryall.

Children love to have their own things just like adults. If you've ever traveled with a child, you know that includes wanting to pack his or her own suitcase. Use ready-made pillowcases to quickly make a kid-sized garment cover and carryall. While they may not hold up to airline travel, they're just right for car trips, sleepovers or a trip to grandma's.

Before sewing, decorate the pillowcases with fabric paint and odds and ends that you have around the house. Prewash the pillowcases and slip them over a piece of cardboard covered with waxed paper on both sides. Look around the house and collect items with interesting shapes and textures to use in the printing process. Things such as empty spools, corks, sponges, hardware items (hex nuts, brackets) will act as stamps and blocks to print onto the fabric. Be sure that the items can easily be picked up by a child's small hands. A paper clip might make an interesting design, but it is so small and thin that it will be hard for a child to put it into paint and pick it up for printing without smearing paint onto the project. The older the child, the better his or her dexterity will likely be and the smaller and thinner the items can be.

To print paint the pillowcases, have the child choose the colors he or she wants. The garment cover and carryall shown in the color section started with red-striped pillowcases and were printed with bright primary colors of paint. Squeeze about a teaspoon of each color of paint onto a paper plate. Choose the item desired and put it into the paint, making sure that the side of the object becomes covered with the paint. Use the object as a stamp on the fabric to apply paint in the shape of the object. To print both sides of the pillowcases, let the first side dry overnight and paint the other side the next day. After completing the painting of the pillowcases, let them dry overnight before beginning to sew.

Garment Cover

DIRECTIONS

1. Turn the pillowcase wrong side out. Trim off the stitched seam opposite the hemmed edge.

2. Find the center of the trimmed edge and measure out 2″ on each side and mark. Do this on both the front and back. Hem the edge of the pillowcase between the markings by folding ¼″ under twice and stitching in place.

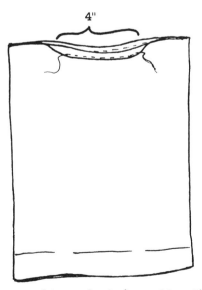

4″

Turn raw edges under twice and topstitch.

3. With the top edges even, lay a clothes hanger on the pillowcase with the hook extending above the edge. Trace along the top of the hanger with a fabric marker. The traced lines should cross the stitched edge to leave an opening of about 1½″.

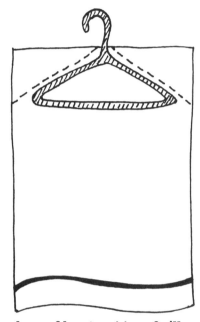

Trace shape of hanger at top of pillowcase.

4. Stitch on the drawn lines, backstitching at the edges to secure the stitching. Trim off the excess fabric about ½″ above the stitching line.

5. Turn the pillowcase right side out and press. The prehemmed edge of the case is the bottom opening of the garment cover. To use, slip over clothes that are on a hanger so that top of hanger comes through the small opening in the top.

Carryall

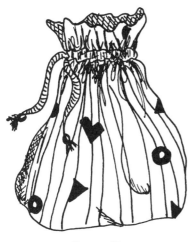

Carryall.

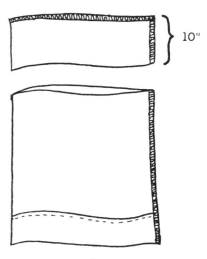

Remove 10″ from top edge of pillowcase.

This tote bag shown in the color section measures 20″ x 17″, however it can be made any size up to the dimensions of the pillowcase.

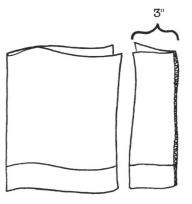

Remove 3″ from seamed side of pillowcase.

MATERIALS

One standard-size pillowcase

1¼ to 1½ yards of cording for drawstring

Thread

Sewing machine

DIRECTIONS

1. Turn the pillowcase wrong side out. Cut 10″ away from the seamed end. Cut 3″ away from the seamed side.

2. Lay the prehemmed edge out flat and remove about 2″ of hem stitching from each of the cut side edges. Fold ½″ of the side raw edges to the inside. Press and stitch. Restitch hem stitching that was removed.

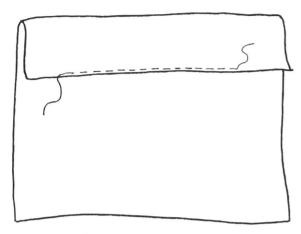

Remove 2″ of stitching at each end of pre-hemmed edge.

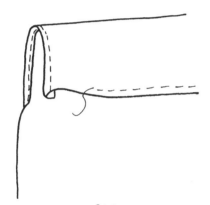

Fold under ¹/₂″ and stitch.

3. Fold with right sides together and stitch across the bottom edge, using a ¹/₂″ seam allowance.

4. To make the casing for the drawstring, measure 1″ from the stitched edge of the hem and sew a straight stitch across the pillowcase. The portion of the hem above the casing will form a header or ruffle. The size of this ruffle will depend on the depth of the hem on the pillowcase.

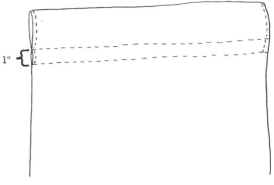

Stitch casing for drawstring.

5. To sew the side seam, use a ¹/₂″ seam allowance and stitch from below the hemmed edge to the bottom seam.

6. To make a flat base on the bottom of the bag, fold the bag so that the seam is flat and a triangle point is formed. Measure 2″ from each point and stitch across at this point. Trim close to the stitching, if desired.

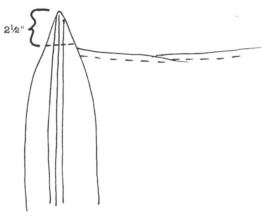

Make a flat base at the bottom of the bag.

7. Thread the cord through the casing and pull up to close the bag.

Ages 3–5

Child can:

- ❑ Choose the paint colors.
- ❑ Help look for and select items with which to paint.
- ❑ Paint one side of the pillowcase (attention span is usually too short to wait for drying to move to second side).
- ❑ Help outline a hanger on the pillowcase for the garment cover.

Ages 6–9

Child can:

- ❑ Choose the paint colors.
- ❑ Look for and select items with which to paint.
- ❑ Paint both sides of the pillowcase, after waiting for the first side to dry.
- ❑ Outline a hanger on the pillowcase for the garment cover and cut on the drawn lines.
- ❑ Cut out the carryall.
- ❑ Sew straight seams with guidance.
- ❑ Thread the drawstring cord through the casing.

Ages 10–12

Child can:

- ❑ Choose the paint colors.
- ❑ Look for and select items with which to paint.

- ❑ Paint both sides of the pillowcase, after waiting for the first side to dry.
- ❑ Outline a hanger on the pillowcase for the garment cover and cut on the drawn lines.
- ❑ Cut out the carryall.
- ❑ Thread the drawstring cord through the casing.

NOTE: Depending on skill level and experience, a child in this age group may be able to complete most of this project with minimal supervision. Help may be required for reworking the hem for the carryall.

Don't forget to pack:

- ❑ toothbrush
- ❑ toothpaste
- ❑ shampoo
- ❑ comb
- ❑ pajamas
- ❑ clean underwear
- ❑ favorite toy

Walk-on sweatshirt.

Walk-On Sweatshirt

The sweatshirt shown in the color section was decorated with a great idea from Jan Dunlap, a Cub Scout leader. It will work for other groups, such as Sunday school classes, day care, and even grandkids.

MATERIALS

Light-colored sweatshirt

Various colors of fabric paint

Shallow pan or plate large enough for the child's foot

Purchased shirtboard or cardboard covered with waxed paper

DIRECTIONS

1. Place the cardboard in the shirt and lay it out flat on the floor.

2. Have the child step in paint with a clean, bare foot. An adult will need to help the child keep his or her balance and place the foot on the shirt. Press down the foot to make the print.

3. After all children have made footprints, paint a saying around them (e.g., I let my grandkids walk all over me!)

Ages 3–5

Child can:

❑ Select the color of paint to use.

❑ Make a footprint with guidance.

49

Ages 6–9

Child can:

- ❏ Select the color of paint to use.
- ❏ Help to prepare the shirt for painting.
- ❏ Make a footprint with assistance.

Ages 10–12

Child can:

- ❏ Complete all steps for the decorated sweatshirt. Will need help with balance while painting footprint.

NOTES

_____

_____

_____

_____

_____

_____

_____

_____

_____

_____

_____

_____

_____

_____

_____

_____

_____

_____

CHAPTER 4

Stitch by Stitch

Learning to manage a hand needle and thread gives children a skill that they will use throughout their entire lives. Sewing on a button or hemming a pair of slacks are simple acts of maintenance that many adults cannot do. The following projects are designed to teach your children the mechanics of hand sewing while having fun and making something useful. Beginning with the Monogrammed Marble Bag, they learn about threading needles and the in-and-out motion of the basic running stitch. As they work through the items, they build on this knowledge and become more involved with the design and embellishment process by learning basic embroidery stitches and simple garment construction.

Managing a needle and thread is a useful skill for anyone to have.

Monogrammed Marble Bag

Monogrammed marble bag.

This simple drawstring bag can hold marbles, jacks, or trinkets of any kind. This project is perfect for a young child or a first-time stitcher. The stitch used is the most basic, the running stitch, and offers a beginner an easy way to get comfortable with a needle and thread.

MATERIALS

12″ square of imitation suede fabric

36″ of yarn, cord, or decorative shoelace to use as a drawstring

Small piece of felt

Thread to match felt

Large needle (for yarn)

Hand sewing needle

Glue stick

Plastic toggle closure (optional)

Pinking shears

Leather or paper hole punch

DIRECTIONS

1. To cut a circle, fold the fabric in half. Fold in half again. Measure 5″ from the double-folded corner (the center of the circle) down both sides. Connect marks with a curved line. Cut on this line with pinking shears and open out the circle.

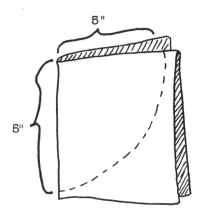

Fold fabric into quarters to measure and cut circle.

2. Choose the desired letter from the monogram patterns. Trace it onto paper and cut it out. Place the letter on felt and draw around the edges. Cut out the drawn letter.

3. Use a glue stick to baste the letter on the right side of the circle. Place the top of the letter about 2″ from the pinked edge of the circle.

4. With matching thread, stitch the letter onto the fabric using a running stitch around the edges. In a running

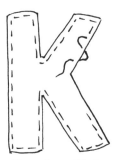

Running stitch.

Make the Memory Quilt and the Cut-Up Cushion (Chapter 2) by decorating swatches of fabric and piecing them together.

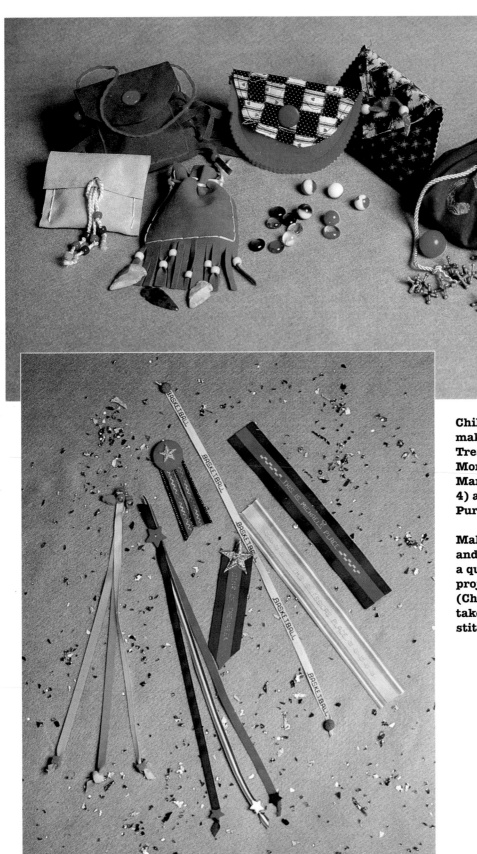

Children will love making these Tiny Treasure Bags and Monogrammed Marble Bag (Chapter 4) and Woven Coin Purses (Chapter 2).

Making bookmarks and award badges is a quick-and-easy project for children (Chapter 2). All it takes is decorative stitching on ribbon.

Laminate your child's original artwork to decorate a notebook cover and totebag (Chapter 3).

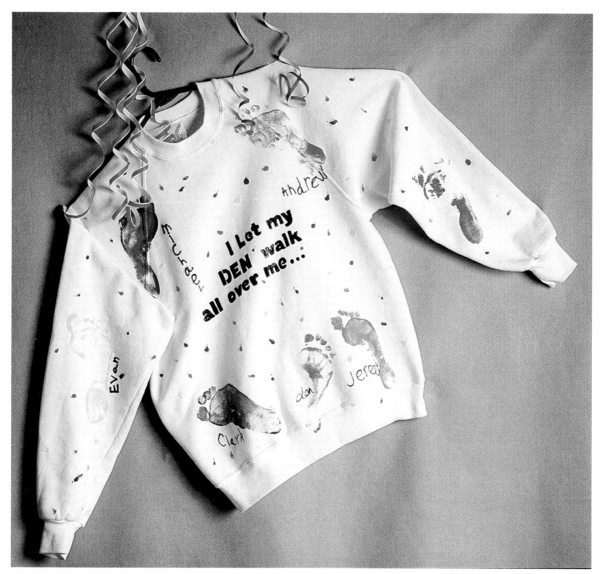

Footprint painting on sweatshirts is fun and easy for even the youngest child (Chapter 3).

Opposite page (top)
Add color to accessories that you make or buy with splashes of paint (Chapter 3).

Opposite page (bottom)
Colorful paper and a little glue are used to create Geometric Jewelry and a Collage Planter (Chapter 5).

Sponge shapes are easy for small hands to paint with. These shirts were painted by a five year old (Chapter 3).

All Occasion cards (Chapter 5) allow children to express special thoughts to the ones they love.

Mini-quilts made by hand (Chapter 5) serve as trivets for hot dishes.

Help your child learn
easy embroidery
stitches to embellish
their Very Own Vest
(Chapter 4).

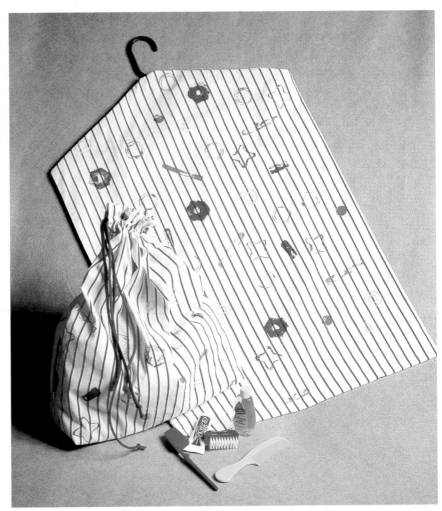

Painted pillowcases
are used to make a
kid-sized garment bag
and carryall
(Chapter 3).

stitch, the needle moves in and out of the fabric in a straight line and equidistance apart. It can be stitched one motion at a time—down into the fabric and out the other side, then up through the fabric and out the top. Another way to stitch it is to place the needle in and out of the fabric several times before pulling it through.

5. Draw a circle 1" from the pinked edge. Punch holes ½" apart around the drawn circle.

6. Thread shoelace, cord, or yarn (threaded through the large needle) through the punched holes with an in-and-out motion similar to a running stitch.

7. Tie a knot in each end of the cord or yarn, or use a cord lock on the ends of the drawstring.

8. With the wrong side up, pull up the drawstring to secure the bag.

Ages 3–5

Child can:

❑ Help to select colors of fabric and felt. Limit the choices to two or three colors and allow him or her to make the final decision.

❑ Glue the letter on to hold it in place for stitching. Help the child position it correctly.

❑ Observe as you stitch the letter and the yarn around the circle to become aware of the in-and-out motion of the needle.

❑ Help in threading the drawstring through the punched holes.

❑ Assist in pulling up the closure to secure the bag and complete the project.

Ages 6–9

Child can:

❑ Make selections of color for fabric and felt. Offer him or her the choice of coordinating the two fabric colors.

❑ Help to fold the square of fabric and make the markings for cutting it into a circle.

❑ Cut out a paper pattern for the monogram and glue the letter in place for stitching. May be able to help measure to find the correct positioning of the letter.

❑ Help with stitching of the letter. Will be able to put the needle in and out of the fabric, one motion at a time. You will need to guide the child through the stitches because of the small size.

❑ Thread the drawstring through the punched holes.

❑ Help to attach closure and secure the bag.

Ages 10–12

Child can:

❑ Accomplish most of the steps involved in this project on his or her own. Will need direction in going from step to step and seeing the project through to the end. May or may not need help in measuring and threading needles.

Mini-Quilt Trivet

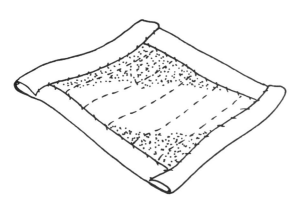

Mini-quilt trivet.

This quilted rug for hot pots is a miniature version of a bed quilt. The front and back fabric is layered with a piece of fleece sandwiched between them. The layers are then quilted together with a running stitch and, to finish off, the edges are "bound" with felt strips. Once a child has completed one of these practical projects, he or she will have an understanding of the basic process it takes to sew a quilt. This is a great gift idea for teachers, grandmothers, and aunts.

MATERIALS

Two 8″ squares of a firmly woven fabric (prewash the fabric before cutting squares)

One 8″ square of fleece

Four strips of felt 2″ x 8″

Needle

Sewing thread

DIRECTIONS

1. Sandwich the fleece between the two squares of fabric. Pin together, keeping the layers as smooth and even as possible.

2. Thread the needle and quilt the layers together using a running stitch (in-and-out motion). Choose one of the stitch patterns illustrated or make up your own.

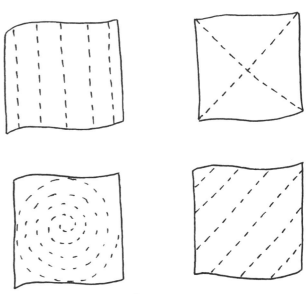

Stitching patterns.

3. Take one strip of felt and place it over one raw edge with 1″ on the fabric and 1″ off the edge. Make sure the ends of the felt strips are even with the ends of the fabric.

4. Using a thread color that matches the felt, whipstitch the felt to the fabric. To whipstitch, pick up a small amount (1–2 threads) of fabric with the needle, then put needle through the felt.

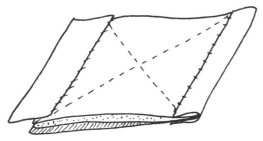

Bind edges with strips of felt.

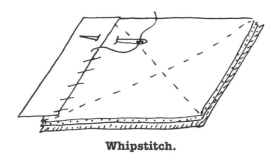

Whipstitch.

5. Wrap the other edge of the felt around to the back of the rug and whipstitch to the fabric.

6. Repeat with a second strip of felt on the opposite edge.

7. Continue, stitching the other two strips of felt to the remaining sides.

TIP: For a scented rug, sprinkle both sides of the fleece with two table-spoons of ground cinnamon before putting the layers together. When a hot pot is placed on the trivet, the warmth will release the pleasant aroma of cinnamon.

Ages 3–5

Child can:

❑ Choose the fabrics and felt from a limited selection.

❑ Sprinkle the cinnamon over the fleece.

❑ Hold the layers of fleece and fabric together while you pin-baste it in place.

❑ Observe as you quilt the layers together to become familiar with the in-and-out motion of the needle. May be able to pull the needle through after you place it in the fabric.

Ages 6–9

Child can:

❑ Select the colors and fabrics desired.

❑ Cut out the felt strips and the squares of fabric and fleece. May need help measuring and marking the 8″ square (or, cut out an 8″ square of plastic or stiff cardboard and the child can use it as a template to draw around).

❑ Sprinkle the cinnamon over the fleece.

❑ Sandwich the fleece between the fabrics.

❑ Pin-baste the layers together. May need help in keeping the layers smooth and even.

❑ Thread the needle and quilt the layers together.

❑ Position the felt and whipstitch it in place. May need some supervision in order to bind the edges evenly.

Ages 10–12

Child can:

❑ Select the colors and fabrics needed for the project.

❑ Measure and cut the felt strips and the 8″ squares of fabric and fleece. (A child in this age group might want to make the project more interesting by piecing coordinating fabrics together to make an 8″ square. The pieced trivet shown in the color section was made with two triangles. Each triangle has two 8¼″ sides and one 10″ side. They are stitched together across the longest side using a ¼″ seam allowance. This can be sewn using very small hand running stitches or on a sewing machine.)

❑ Sandwich the layers together and pin-baste them in place.

❑ Quilt the layers together.

❑ Bind the edges of the rug by whip-stitching the felt strips around the edges.

Tiny treasure bags.

Tiny Treasure Bags

This collection of small leather pouches are easy to make and perfect for holding valuable finds, such as rocks, arrowheads, or coins. The stitch used in these bags is the back-stitch, which gives a sturdy seam that is strong and secure. A back-stitch forms a straight outline stitch that is stronger than a running stitch. The stitch is usually worked from right to left. The needle comes out from behind the fabric at #1, goes in at #2, and back out at #3. Repeat the sequence starting with the needle in at #1 and out at #4. Continue this process until desired stitching is complete.

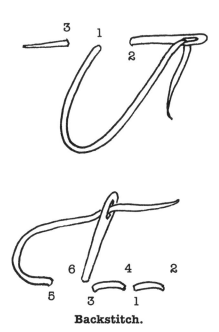

Backstitch.

MATERIALS

Small pieces of real or imitation leather or suede

Embroidery floss or yarn

Small beads (optional)

Awl

Needle

Bag #1

DIRECTIONS

1. Cut one piece of leather 4″ x 4″ for the back and one piece 4″ x 6″ for the front.

2. To form the fringe across the bottom, clip the longer rectangle 2″ in from the bottom at ¼″ intervals.

3. Place the rectangles wrong sides together with the bottom of the smaller rectangle at the top of the fringe.

4. Using the awl, punch holes for stitching. Starting at the top, ¼″ away from the cut edge, make holes ½″ apart.

5. Sew together about ¼″ from the edge along the two sides and the bottom with a backstitch.

Tie a knot in the end of thread after the needle is threaded. When beginning the stitching (at #1), bring the needle up through the top layer only. This will place the knot between the layers of fabric and hide it from view. Continue stitching as described above. At the end of the stitching, put the needle through the top layer of fabric only and tie a knot in it to finish it off. Clip the extra thread so that the end is hidden between the layers of fabric.

To sew around corners, stitch until the needle is at the corner. When coming up through the fabric, bring the needle up through the first hole on the bottom edge and continue stitching as before. This will form a triangular shape on the back of the project at the corner.

6. Make four ½″ slits along the top on the front and four on the back about ½″ from the top edge.

7. Cut the cord or yarn into two equal pieces. Weave one through the slits from each side and pull up to close. If desired, decorate the fringe by sliding beads onto the strands. Tie a knot below the bead, if needed, to keep it from slipping off.

Bag #2

DIRECTIONS

1. Cut one piece of leather 4″ x 9″.

2. Cut a 1½″ slit 1¼″ from each side edge near the center of the piece.

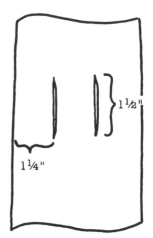

Cut 1½″ slits 1¼″ from each side edge near the center of the piece.

3. With a leather or paper hole punch, put a small hole in the center of the flap, ½″ up from the edge.

4. Cut four pieces of yarn or narrow ribbon 4″ long. Tie knots and/or place beads at random intervals on three of the pieces.

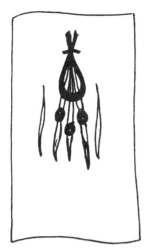

Place beads on three of the yarn pieces. Fold the fourth piece into a loop and place as shown.

5. Fold the fourth piece into a loop and place together as shown.

6. Stitch to the center front of the bag, stitching through the yarn and securing the thread on the inside of the bag.

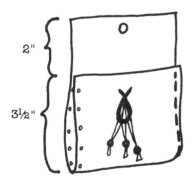

2"

3½"

Fold the lower edge up and sew sides together.

7. Fold the lower edge up and using the awl make holes for stitching ¼" from the sides. Sew the sides together using a backstitch.

8. To close, fold the flap down and pull the loop only through the punched hole. Pull the other strands through the loop.

9. To wear this pouch, place the end of a belt into one of the slits and out the other one.

Treasures to collect:

_____

_____

_____

_____

_____

_____

_____

_____

_____

_____

_____

_____

_____

_____

59

Bag #3

DIRECTIONS

1. Cut two pieces of leather, one 9" x 4" and one 4" x 7".

2. Cut a second piece of leather 4" x 7". Slightly round the corners at one end. To make fringe, cut the sides in 2" every ¼".

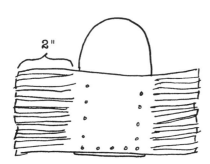

Place fringed piece over flap.

3. Place the two pieces wrong sides together with the fringed piece centered across the lower edge of the other one.

4. Using the awl, punch holes for stitching. Starting at the top, ¼" away from the cut edge, make holes ½" apart. Stitch the bottom and each side along the fringe using a back-stitch.

Stitch cord through flap and tie for handle.

5. Sew a small button in the center of the front of the bag, about ½" down from the edge.

6. Fold the flap down and cut a slit for the button to go through.

7. For a handle or carrying loop, cut 6-strand embroidery floss 36" long and fold in half. Tie one end to a stationary object such as a door knob. Twist tightly and fold in half again, letting it twist together.

8. Thread the end of the twisted floss through a large tapestry needle and knot one end. From the wrong side of the flap, put the needle through the fabric just above the edge of the pouch. Pull through to the knot in the end.

9. Put the needle into the fabric on the other side of pouch, leaving 6" to 8" of slack in the stitch to form a handle. Tie a knot in the end of the cord and trim any excess.

10. Decorate fringe with beads, if desired.

Ages 3–5

Child can:

- ❑ Select the style of treasure bag to make.
- ❑ Choose the color of leather from a limited selection (two or three choices).
- ❑ Choose beads to decorate the fringe, if applicable.
- ❑ Help to twist the cord for the handle loop.
- ❑ Help to slide beads onto the fringe, if applicable.

Ages 6–9

Child can:

- ❏ Decide which style of treasure bag to make.

- ❏ Select the color of leather for the bag.

- ❏ Choose beads for decoration, if applicable.

- ❏ Cut out the rectangles for the chosen bag.

- ❏ Cut slits to make fringe, if applicable.

- ❏ Place the pieces together for stitching. May be able to stitch bags with some direction and supervision.

- ❏ Twist the cord for the handle loop. Will need help getting started and finishing off.

- ❏ Embellish the fringe with beads, if applicable.

Ages 10–12

Child can:

- ❏ Accomplish most of this project alone. Many children in this age group will be able to complete most, if not all, steps of this project. May need some direction and supervision, depending on previous sewing experience. Most will probably need specific directions for the backstitch.

Very Own Vest

This colorful vest is fun and easy to make. It gives the child a chance to be creative and explore the artist within. The stitches used to embellish the front of the vest are basic embroidery stitches and can be translated into other projects as the child's interest and skills progress.

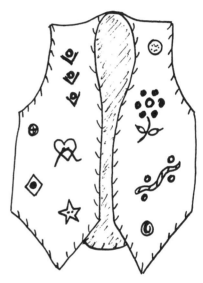

Very own vest.

MATERIALS

Your favorite vest pattern (almost any will work, however one with straight side seams and no darts or seams in the front will be the most simple to use. Select one size larger than normally worn.)

Felt—choose a bright color of washable felt and buy yardage according to the pattern information. Choose a second color for the lining and buy the same amount of yardage. (The vest can be

Comparing notes on each other's vest designs.

made of one layer only—no lining—as the boy's vest with patches shown in the color section.) Prewash according to manufacturer's directions.

Embroidery floss, three to six different colors to coordinate and trim the vest. One skein of each color.

Needle (large-hole needle to accommodate the 6-strand embroidery floss)

Assorted buttons, pins, patches, and trinkets

Chalk or fabric marker

Sewing machine

Iron

DIRECTIONS

1. Prepare the pattern by trimming away the seam allowances (usually ⅝″) at the neck edge, armscye, and lower edge. Do not trim away side seam allowances or shoulder seam allowances.

2. Trim away any front overlap by cutting on the center front line.

3. Overlap the side seam allowances and pin or tape together on the stitching line, creating one large pattern piece.

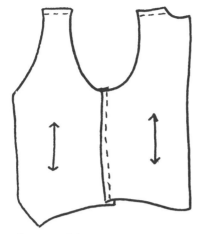

Converting traditional vest pattern to a one-piece version.

4. Using the single pattern piece, cut the vest from one of the pieces of felt.

Carefully cut the vest from the felt.

5. Cut the vest lining from the other piece of felt. Do not cut both the lining and the vest at the same time. They should be exactly the same size, and cutting them together may distort one or both of the layers of felt.

6. Place the shoulder seams of the vest right sides together and stitch using the sewing machine. Trim the edges of the seam allowance at an angle away from the edge of the vest.

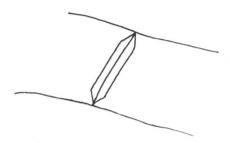

Trim shoulder seams at an angle.

7. Press seams open. Repeat with the lining.

8. Copy the design of the vest shown, or plan your own using buttons and the embroidered shapes illustrated below. Another design option as shown in the color section is to use colorful patches, which can be applied by fusing or machine stitching where desired. Place the vest on a table and arrange buttons, patches, and/or pins across the front. Using chalk or a fabric marker, draw designs to embroider and consider the colors of floss you wish to use.

9. Using six strands of floss, thread a large needle. Stitch your chosen designs by following the directions below.

Starburst. Bring the needle up through the fabric at the center of design (#1), then down at the end of

63

one of the spokes (#2). Come back up at the center (#1) and down at the end of another spoke (#3). Continue this until the design is completed.

point of the needle. Put the needle down at #3, taking a small stitch over the floss.

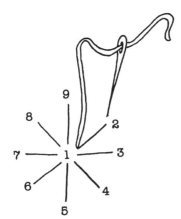

Stitching the starburst pattern.

Outline stitch. This stitch is usually worked from left to right. Bring the needle up from behind the fabric at #1. Take a small stitch at #2, keeping the floss below the needle. After pulling the floss through at #2, move to the right and take another small stitch, again keeping the floss below the needle. Continue until the desired stitching is completed.

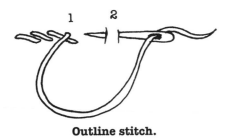

Outline stitch.

Lazy daisy stitch. This stitch is used to give the look of flower petals or leaves. Bring the needle up through the fabric at #1 and put the needle down through the fabric in the same hole (#1). Bring it up at #2, keeping the yarn under the

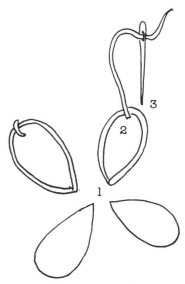

Lasy daisy stitch.

Flying geese. This V-shaped stitch can be worked horizontally or vertically. Bring the needle up at #1 and down into the fabric at #2. Come up at #3 and down again at #4. Move the needle to the beginning of the next V and repeat the stitching sequence. Continue until the desired number of geese are stitched. Embellish with buttons or trinkets, if desired.

Flying geese.

Couching a cord. This applies a decorative cord to the surface of the fabric with a series of small stitches worked over the cord. Lay the cord on the surface of the fabric and bring the needle up from the back close to the side of the cord (#1). Go down into the fabric on the other side of the cord (#2) with the floss going over the cord. Come up at #3, over the cord and down at #4. Continue stitching until the cord is in place. The ends of the cord may be left free or threaded into a large needle and pulled to the back.

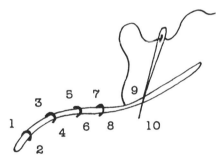

Couching a cord onto the surface of a fabric.

Diamond motif. The diamond motif is a simple design made with four large running stitches. Come up at #1 and down into the fabric at #2. Come back up at #3, which is about ⅛″ away from position #2. Down at #4, up at #5, down at #6, up at #7

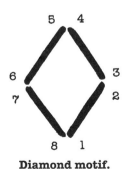

Diamond motif.

and down at #8 will complete the diamond shape. Glue or stitch a button or charm in the center of the diamond to complete the design.

Sewing on buttons. Using embroidery floss or double thread will make sewing the buttons faster and give a stronger hold. Bring the needle up through a hole and down through another. You may stitch across, down, or at a diagonal. Repeat stitching several times and tie off the thread.

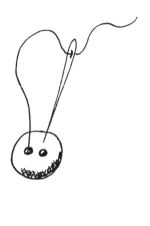

Sewing on buttons.

10. Place the lining and the vest wrong sides together. Pin at various places to hold them together as you stitch. The edges should meet as exactly as possible. If they are slightly uneven, trim to make them even.

11. Mark the placement of the overedge stitching using a template made from paper or plastic. To make a template, cut a strip of stiff paper or lightweight plastic 6″ x 1″. Draw a line across the strip, ½″ from the edge. Mark off 1″ intervals across the strip. Using a hole punch, make a hole at each intersection of the marks you made.

Use a template to evenly mark stitching.

12. Place the template at the edge of the vest and make a mark at each hole. Move the template along the edge until all edges are marked. Include the armsyce and lower edges.

13. To overcast the edges, thread 6-strand embroidery floss in a large needle and tie a knot at the end. Start at the lower side edge and put the needle through the *vest only* at the mark. This will place the knot of the thread between the layers and give a nice finished look. At the next mark, come from the lining side up through both layers and out the top. Continue this around the entire vest.

Overcasting the edges of the vest for the finishing touch.

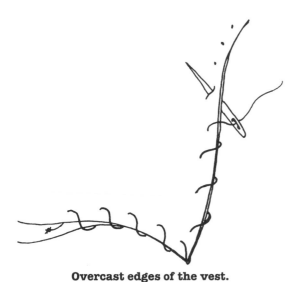

Overcast edges of the vest.

14. If the pattern chosen has any fullness in the back, consider changing the style to a more fitted one by choosing one of the options shown below.

Two tucks with button. Make two small tucks equal distances from each side of the center. Fold each tuck to the side and stitch a decorative button on top.

Pleat with button. Make an inverted pleat at the center of the back. Secure with a decorative button.

Belt loops with ribbon ties. Cut two pieces of narrow ribbon 1½" long. Fold the raw ends under and stitch to the back of the vest waistline equal distances from the center. Cut two pieces of 1" ribbon each 20" long. Stitch to the back waistline near the side. Thread the

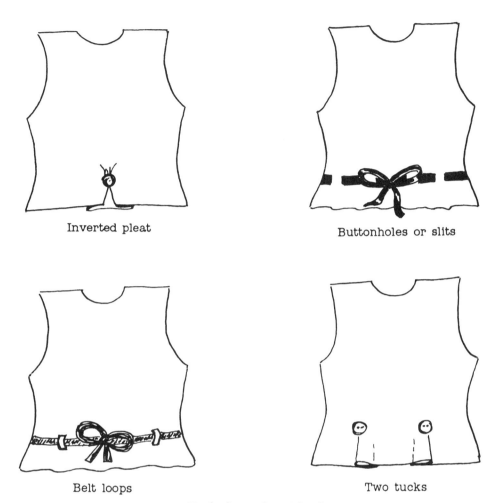

Inverted pleat

Buttonholes or slits

Belt loops

Two tucks

Variations of vest back.

ribbon ties through the loops and tie at the center. Hem the ends of the ribbon or tie into knots.

Slits with ribbon ties. Cut six 1½" slits through both layers of felt (vest and lining) at the waistline of the back. Place them 2" apart. Cut two pieces of 1" ribbon each 20" long. On the wrong side of the vest, stitch the ends of the ribbon near the side at the waistline of the back lining. Thread the ribbon through the slits and tie at the center back. Hem the ends of the ribbon or tie into knots.

TIP: If the vest does not have any extra fullness in the back and you would like to add some, it is a simple matter to do so. When you lay out the pattern, place the center back edge at the fold of the felt. Pivot the lower edge 1" away from the fold, being careful not to displace the neck edge. Pin in place and cut out the vest. After this is done, in order for the vest to fit properly, the back will need to be treated in some way to gather up the extra fullness.

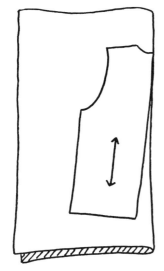

Adding fullness to back of vest.

Ages 3–5

Child can:

- ❑ Help to select the colors of felt from a limited amount of choices.
- ❑ Select the buttons and trinkets to be sewn on the front of the vest.
- ❑ Observe as stitches and buttons are sewn on the front.
- ❑ Assist in marking the edges for overcasting. After you place the template at the edge, have the child mark the holes with a marker.
- ❑ Help in a limited way as edges are being overcast. May be able to pull the needle through the fabric after you have put it in the appropriate place.

Ages 6–9

Child can:

- ❑ Select the color scheme or "theme" for the vest by choosing

felt colors and skeins of embroidery floss.

- ❑ Choose the buttons and trinkets for the front of the vest.
- ❑ Help in the design of the front of the vest. Have the child place the buttons and trinkets in desired place with some design assistance from you. Can also select stitches to complete the look.
- ❑ Thread needles.
- ❑ Stitch some of the simpler designs, such as flying geese, diamond, and starburst with some supervision and guidance.
- ❑ Help with the marking of the overcast stitch on the edges. Will need some direction on how to use the template.
- ❑ Assist with overcasting the edges. You will need to pin the vest and lining together and start the stitching. After watching you, the child should be able to continue stitching. You will need to finish and tie off the thread.

Ages 10–12

Child can:

- ❑ Help in preparing the pattern for the vest. Have the child trim appropriate seam allowances from a tissue pattern.
- ❑ Choose the color scheme or "theme" for the vest by selecting the felt and embroidery floss.
- ❑ Select the button, trinkets, and embroidery stitches for the design on the front of the vest.

❑ Cut out the vest and lining from the felt. Child may need guidance and supervision with the positioning and pinning of the pattern piece.

❑ Design the embellishment for the front of the vest. Child may need some help from you to see some of the possibilities, but should be able to make the decisions of placement and color on his or her own.

❑ Accomplish most, if not all, of the embroidery stitches independently. Will probably need instruction on how the stitch is formed in order to get started.

❑ Sew the buttons, trinkets, and patches onto the front of the vest.

❑ Sew the shoulder seams of the vest and the lining together using the sewing machine.

❑ Put the vest and lining wrong sides together and pin to prepare for stitching. May need help trimming if the two are not exactly the same size.

❑ Mark the placement of the overcast stitching on the edges using the template guide.

❑ Overcast the edges with embroidery floss.

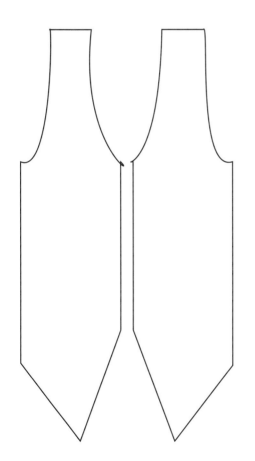

Design your Very Own Vest:

Vest color:

_____

_____

_____

Thread colors:

_____

_____

_____

Favorite stitch design:

_____

_____

_____

CHAPTER 5
Pieces of Paper

Paper is a perfect material for kids' craft projects. It is plentiful, easy to work with, and allows for a myriad of different techniques and end results. Even the youngest child can participate in the crafts shown in this chapter.

MATERIALS

Cardboard box (any size will work; however, for the first project select a smaller one to make it fairly quick to complete)

Several colors of construction paper (small scraps leftover from other projects will work well for this)

White paper glue

Small foam brush (optional)

Clear spray finish

Decorative cord or yarn (optional)

Aluminum foil (to protect the work surface from glue, place aluminum foil over it)

Collage Planter Box

The planter box shown in the color section can also be used as a trinket box or a storage box for crayons, markers, and art supplies. It begins with any cardboard box and is transformed into a collage of color by using torn bits of construction paper. This project is fun for all ages and takes no special or particular skills to complete.

Collage planter box.

One of the attractions of this project is that it allows you to get your hands into it and work it with your fingers. The secret to the success of this project is to use plenty of glue to cement it all together. Keep a damp towel nearby to wipe the glue from your hands periodically.

DIRECTIONS

1. Tear construction paper into irregular shapes with rough edges.

Construction paper torn into irregular shapes.

2. Working on a small area at a time (about 4″ x 4″), spread a thin layer of glue on the surface of the box with the foam brush.

3. Using the brush or your fingers, spread glue onto the backs of pieces of paper and glue each onto the box in a random pattern. Overlap edges and spread colors out in a pleasing arrangement. Be liberal with the glue, spreading any excess over the surface of the paper if needed.

4. Once the entire outer surface of the box is covered, evenly spread a layer of glue over the paper and set aside to dry. Drying time should be at least eight hours.

5. After the box has dried completely, spray with finish, following the directions on the container. Allow the

finish to dry according to manufacturer's directions.

6. If desired, tie a decorative cord or yarn around the box as embellishment.

NOTES

_____
_____
_____
_____
_____
_____
_____
_____
_____
_____
_____
_____
_____
_____
_____
_____
_____
_____
_____
_____
_____
_____
_____
_____
_____

Diamond Necklace

Diamond necklace.

DIRECTIONS

1. Cut four of each of the following size squares: 2″, 1½″, 1″, and ½″.

2. With a hole punch, make a hole in one corner of all of the largest squares.

3. Using a foam brush or your fingers, spread glue evenly on the surfaces of the large squares and stack them together, lining up the holes.

4. Repeat this with each of the other sizes of squares.

5. Layer the differently sized squares by stacking them from large to small as shown. Spread glue evenly across the front of the stacked squares. Let dry.

6. Spray with finish after the glue is dry.

Bright Buttons

Dress up a plain shirt or blouse by putting geometric beacons of color down the front. These brightly colored jewels are created by layering interesting shapes of construction paper and accenting the finished shape with contrasting splashes of paint.

Bright button covers.

MATERIALS

Several colors of construction paper

White paper glue

Small foam brush (optional)

Clear spray finish

Acrylic or fabric paint

Button cover forms (available in fabric stores)

Aluminum foil (to protect the work surface from glue)

DIRECTIONS

1. Cut the appropriate shapes from various colors of construction paper.

2. Spread glue thickly on the back of each shape and stack together 7 to 10 layers of the paper. Allow the shapes to misalign slightly in order to show colors around the edges. Excess glue should be spread evenly over the surface of the button covers. Allow to dry overnight.

Layer squares of construction paper with glue.

3. Paint squiggles and dots on the front of the glued shapes.

Add interest with bits of paint.

4. Spray with a high-gloss finish. Let dry according to the manufacturer's directions.

5. Glue button cover forms to the back of the shapes.

Glitter Pin

This flashy pin sparkles to add glamour to any outfit.

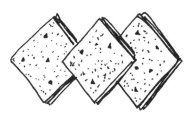

Glitter pin.

MATERIALS

Several colors of construction paper

White paper glue

Small foam brush (optional)

Clear spray finish

Scissors

Aluminum foil (to protect the work surface from glue)

Pin back

Glitter

DIRECTIONS

1. Cut out 15 to 20 1″ squares of brightly colored paper.

2. Make three stacks of squares, randomly mixing colors.

3. Using a liberal amount of glue, glue the layers together and let dry thoroughly.

4. Overlap the stacks as shown and glue in place.

5. Spray with a clear finish. Sprinkle glitter over the surface while the finish is still wet. Let dry.

6. Glue the pin back to the back of the shape.

Ages 3–5

Child can:

❑ Select the colors of construction paper and paint.

❑ Choose the desired shapes for button covers.

❑ Spread glue on the back of paper shapes and layer them together.

❑ Paint dots of color on the front of glued shapes.

❑ Sprinkle glitter.

Ages 6–9

Child can:

❑ Select the colors of construction paper and paint.

❑ Choose the desired shapes for button covers.

❑ Spread glue on the back of paper shapes and layer them together.

❑ Paint dots of color on the front of glued shapes.

❑ Glue button cover forms onto the backs of glued shapes.

❑ Sprinkle glitter.

Ages 10–12

Child can:

❑ Select colors of construction paper and paint.

❑ Choose desired shapes for button covers.

❑ Spread glue on the back of paper shapes and layer them together.

❑ Paint dots of color on the front of glued shapes.

❑ Glue button cover forms onto the backs of glued shapes.

❑ Spray with clear finish and sprinkle glitter.

NOTE: Children in this age group will be able to complete much of this project on their own after some having basic direction and instruction given to them.

Carnival Cards

Send these cheerful cards for any occasion. Made from bits of fabric and colorful cardstock or construction paper, the designs are fused to the paper and then embellished and accented with paint, buttons, ribbons, and other items. The directions and patterns are for the cards shown in the color section, however any type of card with any design can be made, so have fun coming up with your own.

MATERIALS

Construction paper or lightweight cardstock in any color desired (If the color is too dark to show writing on the inside of the card, cut a piece of white paper ½" smaller than the card around all four sides. This will be glued to the inside of the card to allow space for a note to be written.)

Small scraps of fabric

Paper-backed fusible web

Iron

Paint, buttons, ribbons, charms, glitter for embellishment

Markers

Christmas Card

Christmas card.

DIRECTIONS

1. Cut paper 12" x 8". Fold it in half across the 8" side.

2. Press paper-backed fusible web to the wrong side of a piece of fabric large enough for the wreath pattern.

3. Draw a wreath onto the paper on the back of the fabric. Cut out the shape using pinking shears.

4. Peel the paper from the back of the wreath and fuse onto the folded card. Use a press cloth to protect the paper from the iron.

5. Make a bow from narrow ribbon. Glue it in place at the bottom of the wreath. Add glitter or sequins on the wreath if desired.

6. Using a marker, write any appropriate holiday message.

Birthday Card

Birthday greetings.

DIRECTIONS

1. Cut card 6" x 13". Fold in half across the 13" side.

2. Fuse paper-backed web to the wrong side of three coordinating fabrics.

3. Using the pattern piece, draw a balloon onto the paper on back of the fabrics. Cut out the drawn shapes.

4. Peel the paper from the back of the balloons and fuse onto the upper left side on the front of the folded card.

5. With a marker, draw the strings from the bottom of the balloons to come together near the lower edge.

6. Tie a bow using narrow ribbon and glue it in place where the strings come together.

7. Place an accent of white paint on each balloon in the upper right area as shown.

8. Using a marker, write "Happy Birthday" on the right side of the card.

9. To make the confetti background, use several colors of markers to randomly place small squares and triangles across the front of the card. With a black marker, fill in the rest of the background with dots of ink.

Special Birthdays to remember:

_____

_____

_____

_____

_____

_____

_____

_____

_____

_____

_____

_____

_____

_____

_____

_____

_____

_____

_____

_____

All-Occasion Star Card

All occasion star card.

DIRECTIONS

1. Cut card 4" x 8".

2. Fuse paper-backed fusible web to the wrong side of fabric pieces large enough for the star patterns.

3. Trace around the star patterns on the back of the fabric. Cut out stars.

4. Place stars across the front of the card as desired. Peel paper from the back and fuse in place.

5. Use glitter glue or brush a thin layer of glue across the stars where glitter is desired. Sprinkle glitter over the glue. Let dry and shake off excess glitter.

Valentine Card or Love Note

Valentine love card.

DIRECTIONS

1. Cut card 6" x 8". For the card shown, black was chosen; therefore, a white liner (½" smaller than the card on all four sides) was glued inside on which to write a message.

2. Press paper-backed fusible web to the back of several small pieces of coordinating fabric. Trace the large heart onto the paper on back of the fabric. Trace the smaller hearts for inside the card onto the paper on the back of coordinating fabric. Cut out hearts.

3. Peel the paper from the back of the hearts and fuse in place on the front of the card.

4. Slip two 5" strands of ribbon through the holes of a button. Tie together. Tie knots in random places along the ribbon ties. Glue the button in place on the heart on the front of the card.

Place white liner in dark cards for writing.

5. Glue a white paper liner in place inside the card, centering it from side to side and top to bottom.

6. Place smaller hearts on the inside overlapping the edges of the liner.

Who will be my Valentine?

_____

_____

_____

_____

_____

_____

_____

_____

_____

_____

_____

_____

_____

_____

_____

Thank-You Note

Happy clown thank you card.

DIRECTIONS

1. Cut card 12″ x 7″.

2. Press paper-backed fusible web onto the back of small scraps of chosen fabrics.

3. Trace pattern pieces for the head, hair, and collar of the clown onto the paper on the back of the appropriate pieces of fabric. Cut out the pieces of the clown.

4. Peel the paper from the back of the cut pieces. Arrange in place on the front of the card and fuse in place.

5. Glue small buttons or moveable eyes in place on the face of the clown.

6. Using markers, draw the nose and mouth as desired.

7. Tie ribbons into a bow tie and glue in place.

Ages 3–5

Child can:

- ❏ Select the color of cardstock from a limited number of choices.

- ❏ Choose shapes and fabrics to be fused onto the cardstock, again from a limited number (2–3) of choices.

- ❏ Help to peel paper from the back of cut-out shapes.

- ❏ Assist in arranging shapes on the front of the card.

- ❏ Help in placing and gluing buttons, ribbons, and embellishments to the design.

- ❏ Add to the design by drawing with markers when needed.

Ages 6–9

Child can:

- ❏ Select the desired design to be made or create an original design.

- ❏ Choose the color of cardstock and specific fabrics and embellishments to be used.

- ❏ Fuse bonding material to the back of the fabric pieces. (Must have adult instruction and close supervision when using the iron.)

- ❏ Trace around the pattern pieces on the back of the fabric.

- ❏ Cut out simple shapes drawn on the back of the fabric.

- ❏ Position the shapes on the front of the card and, with help, fuse them into place.

- ❏ Glue extra embellishment items, such as buttons, ribbons, beads, to the front of the card.

- ❏ Write appropriate messages and draw any additional designs needed on the card.

Ages 10–12

Child can:

- ❏ Select the desired design or create an original design.

- ❏ Choose the color of cardstock and specific fabrics and embellishments to be used.

- ❏ Fuse bonding material to the back of the fabric pieces.

- ❏ Trace around the patterns and cut out shapes.

- ❏ Position the shapes on the front of the card and fuse them into place.

- ❏ Glue extra embellishment items to the front of the cards.

- ❏ Write appropriate message and draw additional designs needed on the card.

Note: Child in this age group should be able to complete all steps needed to make a card. Will need instruction on using the paper-backed bonding material and should be supervised while using the iron.

Textured Paper Ornaments

Textured paper ornament.

Making these paper gift tags, ornaments, and party favors from scratch is not only fun for kids to do, but it teaches them the importance of reusing and recycling whenever possible. Taking old newspapers and turning them into decorative, useful products is a good way to introduce children to the concept of making something new for virtually nothing. These pretty shapes can be creatively painted and decorated and used as gift tags or ornaments.

MATERIALS

Blender

Two to three single pages of newspapers

Small embroidery hoop, cookie cutters, or molds

Two pieces of felt, at least 8″ x 10″ each

Four to five cups of water

Towel

Extra pages of newspaper, about 1″ thick

Cup

Acrylic paint and brush

Assorted ribbons, buttons, charms, silk flowers, glitter for embellishing painted ornament

Craft glue

DIRECTIONS

1. Tear the two to three pages of newspaper into small squares about 1″ to 2″.

2. Place the small pieces of paper in the blender with 4 to 5 cups of water. Process the paper and water for one to two minutes until it is a thick pulp mixture, about the consistency of oatmeal.

3. Place the additional newspapers on a flat, hard, waterproof surface such as a kitchen countertop. Put one piece of felt on top of the newspapers and position the hoop or cookie cutters on the felt.

4. Using a cup, scoop the pulp mixture from the blender and place in the hoop or cookie cutter. With your fingers, spread it around as evenly as possible. Put as much pulp into the frame as desired. The more pulp that is put into the frame, the thicker the shape will be and the longer it will take to dry. As the pulp is spread into the frame, most of the water should soak into the newspaper underneath, but keep the towel handy just in case.

Put paper pulp in a cookie cutter to form shapes.

5. After the excess water has drained, carefully remove the hoop or cookie cutter. Place the second piece of felt over the pulp. Using the towel, soak up as much of the remaining moisture as possible. Take care to blot the moisture and do not push or pull the paper shape, as it is fragile at this point.

6. Remove the top piece of felt to expose the newly made paper shape. Lift the bottom piece of felt and the shape off of the newspaper and set aside to allow the paper to dry. This will take some patience as it may take one to two days to dry completely, depending on the thickness of the shape.

7. Once the pulp is dry, carefully peel the shape from the felt.

NOTE: Leftover pulp should be discarded in the trash; *do not pour it down the drain.* Pulp can be kept for several weeks for use at a later time. Drain any excess water from the left-over pulp and store the pulp in a plastic bag or container in the refrigerator. If it's too dry when you go back to it, add enough water to restore the soft consistency needed.

8. After the shape is completely dry, use acrylic paint to decorate it as desired. Because of the ink in the newspaper, the dry shape will be a light gray color. To get true colors, paint the entire ornament (front and back) white as a base coat before using colors on it.

9. Using craft glue, embellish the ornament with ribbons, buttons, charms, flowers, glitter, as desired.

10. Thread a large needle with six strands of embroidery floss or a $1/8''$ ribbon. Stitch through the paper near the top center of the shape. Cut the floss or ribbon about 8″ to 12″ long and tie together to form a hanging loop.

Ages 3–5

Child can:

- ❑ Tear newspaper pages into small squares and add them to the water in the blender.
- ❑ Push the button on the blender to process the paper and water mixture.
- ❑ Help to pour the pulp mixture into the hoop or cookie cutter.
- ❑ Help to soak up extra water with a towel when the pulp is between the layers of felt.
- ❑ Peel the dried shape from the felt.

❑ Choose the colors of paint for decorating the shapes.

❑ Select ribbons, flowers, and charms for embellishment and help to glue them in place.

Ages 6–9

Child can:

❑ Measure the water and pour it into the blender.

❑ Tear newspaper pages into small squares and add them to the water in the blender.

❑ Operate the blender to process the paper and water mixture.

❑ Pour the pulp mixture into the hoop or cookie cutter and spread it evenly.

❑ Soak up extra water with a towel when the pulp is between the layers of felt.

❑ Peel the dried shape from the felt.

❑ Paint the paper shapes in colors and design of choice.

❑ Decorate the paper shapes with ribbons, flowers, charms, glitter.

Ages 10–12

Child can:

❑ Measure the water and pour it into the blender.

❑ Tear newspaper pages into small squares and add them to the water in the blender.

❑ Operate the blender to process the paper and water mixture.

❑ Pour the pulp mixture into the hoop or cookie cutter and spread it evenly.

❑ Soak up extra water with a towel when the pulp is between the layers of felt.

❑ Remove the top piece of felt and place the wet paper to dry.

❑ Peel the dried shape from the felt.

❑ Paint the paper shapes in colors and design of choice.

❑ Decorate the paper shapes with ribbons, flowers, charms, glitter.

NOTES

_____
_____
_____
_____
_____
_____
_____
_____
_____
_____
_____
_____
_____
_____
_____
_____

Fancy Fan

Have fun and keep cool by making this fan from lightweight cardboard. Dress it up with a pretty adhesive-backed patterned vinyl such as Contact paper. The blades of the fan are held together by lacing ribbon or yarn through the edges and ending in a pretty bow.

MATERIALS

Lightweight cardboard or poster-board, 11" x 14"

Adhesive-backed patterned vinyl, enough to cover both sides of the cardboard

One yard ¼" wide ribbon or yarn in a color that coordinates with the patterned vinyl

Large hand tapestry needle

Paper hole punch

DIRECTIONS

1. Cover both sides of the cardboard with the adhesive-backed patterned vinyl, carefully smoothing the surface to avoid any bubbles or wrinkles.

2. Cut two outside blades according to pattern piece A. Using a hole punch, punch holes at the indicated places.

3. Cut four inside blades according to pattern piece B. Using a hole punch, punch holes at the indicated places.

4. Stack all the blades on top of each other with outside blades on the top and bottom. The holes along the sides on these blades should be along the outside edges of the fan as shown in the illustration. Line up all of the single holes at the bottom of the blades.

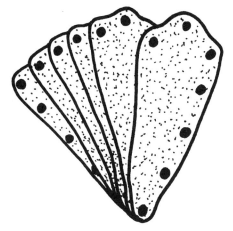

Line up all of the single holes at the bottom of the blades.

5. Thread a needle with ribbon and come up through all of the holes at the bottom of the blades. Pull the ribbon through until about 10" is hanging below the fan.

NOTE: For smaller hands, use tape on the ends of the ribbon instead of threading it through a needle. Wrap a piece of transparent tape around one end of the ribbon, tapering it to a point. This stiffened point will be easier than a needle for small hands to handle.

6. Using an overcast type of motion, coming up from the bottom and over the top, thread the ribbon through the holes along one side of the fan. Straighten the ribbon and keep it laying flat as you sew. Occasionally you should hold up the fan and let the ribbon hang free to allow it to untwist. Work your way across the top

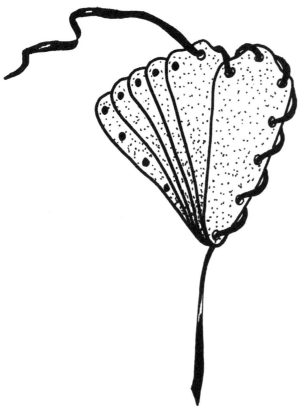

**Thread needle with ribbon and come up
through all of the holes.**

of the fan, overlapping the blades and lining up the side holes on the upper edge. Hold the blades together to begin the stitching and fan each blade out as you come to it, aligning the top side holes of the adjacent blades.

7. After working your way around the fan, thread the ribbon back through the aligned holes at the bottom of the blades. Tie the ribbon into a bow to finish off the fan. Cut the ends of the ribbon at a slant or tie into a knot to keep it from fraying.

NOTE: Children in this age group will be able to complete much of this project on their own after receiving basic directions and instructions.

CHAPTER 6
Kitchen Clay

A favorite pastime of most children is playing and crafting with clay. The soft clay squishes through their fingers and can be shaped into balls and rolled into snakes. For some children, just manipulating and playing with the clay can be more fun than actually making a lasting object; shaping the form and smashing it flat is their idea of great fun. Working with clay helps children to learn about shapes and forms, spacial concepts, textures, and surfaces. And the beauty of it is that the children think they're just having fun!

Crafting with clay can be a messy activity so plan for it before you start. Cover the work surface with a smooth vinyl tablecloth or use an old wooden or acrylic cutting board on which each child can sculpt. Keep a damp towel handy for periodic cleaning of the hands, if needed. This may keep the clays from becoming sticky as they are being formed. These clays require little or no cooking and even young children can help with the measuring and mixing. In fact, all of the clay recipes in this chapter are great for introducing a child to basic measuring methods used in cooking processes.

Acrylic modeling compounds are available at craft and hobby stores and are used for making today's popular jewelry, buttons, and beads. If you are one of the many crafters who enjoys using these compounds, you are probably aware that besides being somewhat costly, they are usually not recommended for children under eight years of age. Fortunately, there are many clays and compounds that can be made in your own kitchen that will work well and cost only pennies. Kitchen clays are simple to make and usually take ingredients that you may already have on hand. The clays will keep for a few weeks if kept in a tightly sealed plastic bag or container in the refrigerator. To use a compound after refrigerating, bring it back to room temperature and knead it to make it soft and workable once again.

Items made from these clays will air dry in one to two days, depending on the thickness. Carefully turn the objects over occasionally for more even drying. When completely dry, the items can be sprayed lightly with a clear acrylic finish. To make colorful sculptures without painting, add food coloring or tempera paint to the clay mixture as it is being mixed or kneaded. When using this method, color the amount you need as you are working with it. Add tempera paint to clay by dipping a craft stick into the paint jar and applying the paint to the clay. Using your fingers, work the paint into the clay until the color is evenly distributed. If the clay begins to get sticky, add a small amount of flour and continue to knead in the color.

Older children may enjoy working with a marbled clay, combining two or more colors in one compound. This technique works best with food coloring rather than paint. Lightly knead a few drops of one color into the clay until veins of color are streaked throughout. If desired, add another color and knead slightly to distribute. Overworking will make the compound a solid color, so work the clay only briefly to mix the colors.

The following recipes offer several options for making clays that work well for the projects in this chapter. Each clay has its own characteristics and you should choose the one that works best for you. Check your cupboard to see which ingredients you have on hand to mix up some fun!

FLOUR CLAY

2 cups all-purpose flour

½ cup salt

¾ cup water

Mix flour and salt together in a bowl. Add a small amount of water and stir until mixed. Continue adding water until a stiff dough is formed. Turn out onto a bread board or a smooth surface and knead until it is smooth, adding a little flour or water if needed.

This clay is soft and smooth and can be colored with tempera paint or food coloring. Tint the clay darker than the desired finished color because it will fade to a lighter shade as it dries. If left untinted, this clay will dry to an off-white color.

BAKING SODA CLAY

2 cups baking soda

1 cup cornstarch

$1\frac{1}{3}$ cups water

Combine all ingredients in a saucepan and cook over medium heat. Stir constantly until the mixture bubbles and gets thick. Turn out onto a plate or cutting board and cover with a damp cloth until cool. This is a soft clay with a smooth texture. Left plain, it dries white and may be painted. When colored with tempera paint or food coloring, it dries to a light pastel shade.

SALT CLAY

2 cups salt

1 cup cornstarch

$1\frac{1}{3}$ cups water

Combine all ingredients in a saucepan and cook over medium heat. Stir constantly until the mixture bubbles and gets thick. Turn out onto a plate or cutting board and cover with a damp cloth until cool. This clay has a grainier texture than the baking soda clay, but it also dries white and can be painted. When colored with paint or food coloring, it will dry fairly true to the original color you made the clay. When dry, it has a slightly rough texture to the touch.

BREAD CLAY

1 slice white bread

1 tablespoon white glue

Remove the crust from the slice of white bread. Discard or save to feed to the birds. Tear the rest of the bread into small pieces. Place them in a small bowl or on a piece of waxed paper and add the white glue. Knead with your fingers until smooth. This is a fairly stiff clay and works better for older children, ages 7 and up. When colored, the clay dries bright with a plastic-like look. Because this clay is stiffer, it can be rolled into thinner snakes and can be used to make smaller and more detailed beads than the softer clays. It can also be rolled out flat, cut, and shaped much like the more expensive plastic modeling clays.

Modeling Projects
Beads

Beads are fun to make and can be used for a variety of projects. Shop at the local craft stores for jewelry findings to make earrings, pendants, button covers, and all types of ornamental items. Beads can be interesting to collect and Cub Scouts even use them for awards and recognition of achievement. Experiment with different ways to make them, and remember, beads are not always round. They can be long, square, flattened, or just about any shape you want.

Beads are fun to make and can be any shape you want.

MATERIALS

Clays in colors of your choice

Smooth work surface

Small dowel or skewer

Round Beads

DIRECTIONS

1. Pull off a small amount of clay and roll it between your hands or on the work surface until it is round and smooth. Beads may be made in various sizes; however, ones larger than 1″ in diameter may crack as they dry.

2. Use the dowel or skewer to make a hole completely through the bead. If planning to string the beads for a necklace or bracelet, the hole needs to be large enough to allow the cord or yarn to pass through.

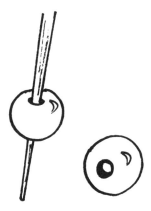

Use a dowel or skewer to make a hole through the bead.

Striped Beads

DIRECTIONS

1. Pull off a small amount of clay and roll it between your hands or on the work surface until it is round and smooth.

2. To add one or more stripes to the bead, roll another color of clay into a very thin snake, about the size of a pencil lead. Wrap the snake around the bead as desired.

Striped bead.

3. Roll the bead between your palms until the stripe blends in. Be careful not to flatten the bead too much or to blend the colors.

4. Use the dowel or skewer to make a hole completely through the bead. If planning to string the beads for a necklace or bracelet, the hole needs to be large enough to allow the cord or yarn to pass through.

Tricolor Beads

Tri-color beads.

MATERIALS

Clay of choice (three different colors)

Smooth work surface

Small dowel or skewer

DIRECTIONS

1. Start with a small amount (about a 1″ to 1½″ ball) of three different colors of clay. Roll each ball into a snake about ¼″ thick. The thickness of the snakes does not have to be consistently even.

2. Lay the snakes side by side and lightly press together at one end. Braid the three snakes together. The braiding does not have to be evenly spaced or perfectly done.

3. Roll the braid gently to make a tricolored snake. Stop after a few seconds to see if you like the results. Be careful not to roll too roughly or too long or the colors will blend together and they will not be three distinct colors.

4. Using a craft knife or a kitchen knife, cut the rolled braid into various sizes. These pieces of braid can be made into beads by using a dowel or skewer to make a hole through the clay. For a different style of bead, slightly flatten the clay piece before making the holes for stringing. To make buttons, flatten the clay pieces more and make two holes for sewing the buttons onto a garment. These can also be glued to button covers and used over existing buttons.

Ages 3–5

Child can:

❑ Pour measured ingredients into the mixing bowl.

❑ Choose the colors for clay and help to work the colors into the clay.

❑ Roll the clay into balls and snakes.

❑ Help to string finished beads to make a necklace or bracelet. Make large holes for very young hands.

Ages 6–9

Child can:

❑ Help to measure and mix the ingredients for the clay.

❑ Make the uncooked clay with some supervision. Stirring may be a bit difficult because of the stiffness of the clay.

❑ Choose the colors for the clay and work them into the clay.

❑ Roll the clay into balls, snakes, and other shapes.

❑ Make the holes in the beads with careful supervision while using any sharp tools.

❑ String beads onto a cord or yarn to make a necklace or bracelet.

Ages 10–12

Child can:

❑ Measure and mix the ingredients for the clay.

❑ Make any of the clays; however, the cooked versions should be supervised.

❑ Choose the colors for the clay and work them into the clay.

❑ Roll the clay into balls, snakes, and other shapes.

❑ Make detailed and intricate designs on the beads.

❑ Make the holes in the beads with careful supervision while using any sharp tools.

❑ String beads onto a cord or yarn to make a necklace or bracelet.

Multicolor Cutouts

These cutout shapes can be used to make pins, refrigerator magnets, pendants, or figurines. Any of the clay mixtures will work for this, depending on if you want a smooth (bread or baking soda clay) or rough (salt clay) surface to the finished project.

MATERIALS

Clay in three or more colors

Smooth work surface (cardboard covered with waxed paper works well)

Cookie cutters and other plastic toy shapes to use as cutouts

Pencil or small dowel

Craft knife (optional)

DIRECTIONS

1. Roll out small lumps (about ½" in diameter) of several colors of clay. These do not need to be rolled until smooth.

Roll out small lumps of different colored clay.

2. Place the lumps so that they are touching in a random pattern of colors.

3. Using a pencil or dowel, roll the clay until it is about ⅛" thick.

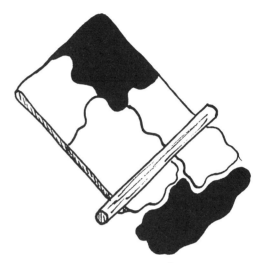

Roll the clay until it is ⅛" thick.

4. Using cookie cutters or plastic toy shapes, cut out desired pieces. Instead of using cutters, you may use a craft knife to cut your own abstract shapes.

Use cookie cutters or a craft knife to create different shapes.

5. After cutting out the shapes, they may be further embellished by creat-

93

ing textures on their surfaces. Many kitchen utensils will make interesting designs; the ends of a pastry brush, the ridges of a honey dipper, the ends of chopsticks, the wire mesh of a tea strainer, and even the pile of a terry cloth hand towel will make an impression on the clay.

6. If planning to make the shape into a pendant, use a small dowel (pencil, chopstick, etc.) to make a hole near the top. This will allow the clay pendant to be threaded onto a cord or chain for wearing.

My favorite color combinations:

_____

_____

_____

_____

_____

_____

_____

_____

_____

_____

_____

_____

_____

_____

_____

_____

Picture Frame

Kitchen clay picture frame.

The multicolored technique can also be used to make a picture frame. Make a frame for the child's school photo and use for exchanging with friends or make it into a refrigerator magnet for Grandma.

MATERIALS

Clay in three or more colors

Smooth work surface (cardboard covered with waxed paper works well)

Craft-knife

Pencil or small dowel

Lightweight cardboard or poster-board

White craft glue

DIRECTIONS

1. Roll out small lumps (about ½″ in diameter) of several colors of clay. These do not need to be rolled until smooth.

2. Place the lumps so that they are touching in a random pattern of colors.

3. Using a pencil or dowel, roll the clay until it is about ⅛″ thick.

4. To make a pattern for the frame, cut a cardboard rectangle the size of the frame you want. Cut an opening in the center of the cardboard pattern slightly smaller than the photograph you are framing.

5. Using the pattern and a craft knife, cut out the frame from the rolled-out clay. Allow to dry. If desired, the frame can be painted or sprayed with an acrylic sealer.

6. Cut a piece of lightweight cardboard about ¼″ smaller than the frame. The frame may shrink slightly while drying, so do this step when the frame is completely dry. Glue the photograph to the cardboard, centering it from side to side and top to bottom. Glue the frame to the cardboard so that the photograph is centered in the frame opening.

7. If desired, glue a magnet to the cardboard on the back of the frame to make a refrigerator decoration.

Ages 3–5

Child can:

❑ Choose the colors and help to work them into the clay.

❑ Arrange small pieces of clay and help to roll them out.

❑ Place and press cookie cutters to make shapes. Adult will need to help remove the shape from the cookie cutter.

❑ Create interesting texture on the surface of the cutout.

Ages 6–9

Child can:

❑ Help to measure and mix the clay ingredients. May need help in stirring the stiffer mixtures.

❑ Choose the colors and work them into the clay.

❑ Arrange small pieces of clay and roll them out.

❑ Use cookie cutters to make cutouts.

❑ Cut abstract shapes and picture frame using a craft knife with close supervision.

❑ Create interesting texture on the surface of the cutout.

Ages 10–12

Child can:

❑ Help to measure and mix the clay ingredients.

❑ Make the cooked clays with some supervision.

❑ Choose the colors and work them into the clay.

❑ Arrange small pieces of clay and roll them out.

❑ Use cookie cutters to make cutouts.

❑ Cut abstract shapes and picture frame using a craft knife with supervision.

❑ Create interesting texture on the surface of the cutout.

NOTE: Children in this age group should be able to complete the cutout projects with a minimum of supervision.

95

Molded Figures

Charms, refrigerator magnets, pins, decorations, and party favors are easy to make using candy molds. They come in a wide variety of shapes, from holiday motifs to dinosaurs to sporting designs. The salt clay made with cornstarch works best for this and releases well from the mold when it is dry. It will take about 24 hours to dry enough to pop it out of the mold. The other clays do not dry well in the plastic candy molds.

MATERIALS

Clay of any desired color

Plastic candy mold

Glitter (optional)

DIRECTIONS

1. Pull off a small section of the clay. If desired, add sparkle to the clay by working in a small amount of glitter. Knead the glitter into the clay until it is evenly distributed throughout the amount you're working with.

2. Fill one section of the mold with the clay. Press the clay down and be sure that it fills all the crevices of the design.

3. Use the edge of a knife to remove any excess clay on the open side of the mold.

4. Allow to dry for 24 hours.

5. Carefully push the mold to remove the clay shape. The clay will still be slightly soft, so handle it carefully to avoid distorting it.

6. If using the molded shape as a pendant or charm, it is necessary to make a loop for a cord or chain to go through. Bend a paper clip open and clip off the rounded end with wire cutters. Insert this rounded end into the top of the clay shape while it is still moist.

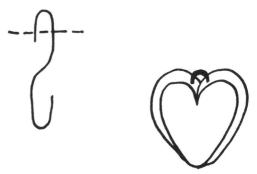

Use a paper clip to make a loop for a cord or a chain to go through.

7. Let the completed shape dry until hard.

Ages 3–5

Child can:

❑ Choose the colors and work them into the clay.

❑ Add glitter and work it throughout the clay.

❑ Help to press the clay into the candy mold.

❑ Thread the completed pendant onto a cord.

Ages 6–9

Child can:

- ❑ Help to measure and mix the clay ingredients.
- ❑ Choose the colors and work them into the clay.
- ❑ Add glitter and work it throughout the clay.
- ❑ Press the clay into the candy mold.
- ❑ Help to release the partially dried shape from the mold.
- ❑ Add a wire loop to the top of the shape.
- ❑ Thread the completed pendant onto a cord.

Ages 10–12

Child can:

- ❑ Measure and mix the clay ingredients.
- ❑ Make the cooked clays with some supervision.
- ❑ Choose the colors and work them into the clay.
- ❑ Add glitter and work it throughout the clay.
- ❑ Press the clay into the candy mold.
- ❑ Release the partially dried shape from the mold.
- ❑ Add a wire loop to top of the shape.
- ❑ Thread the completed pendant onto a cord.

My Room Doorknob Hanger

If a man's home is his castle, then a child's castle is his or her room. A personalized doorknob hanger will let everyone in the house know who lives inside. The hanger can be decorated with a sculpture of the child or with motifs relating to a particular interest, such as sports or space. Special themes could be used for different times of the year to decorate for the holidays or celebrate the seasons. The clay shapes are made and then glued to the cardboard hanger. Use markers, stickers, fabric, and other embellishments to complete the design. The directions that follow are for the self-sculpture design.

MATERIALS

Lightweight cardboard or posterboard

Glass or other round object (to trace circles)

Clay (colored for desired skin color)

Paints

Acrylic sealer

Glue

Scissors

Fabric scraps

Buttons, bows, etc. for clothing embellishment

Construction paper (optional)

A variety of door knob hangers.

DIRECTIONS

1. For the hanger cut a rectangle of cardboard 4″ x 11″.

2. Measure down from the top edge of the rectangle about 1″ to 1½″. Use a glass or other round object to trace a circle about 2½″ in diameter. The circle should be centered between the side edges of the rectangle. Using scissors or a craft knife, cut out the circle.

3. To make the face, roll or pat clay to about ¼″ thick. Cut a 3″ circle using a cookie cutter, a glass, or a can as a pattern. Using small snakes and balls, make hair, eyes, nose, mouth, and ears. Add extras, such as glasses and hair bows. Apply these features to the face and press slightly to attach.

4. Allow to dry thoroughly. Paint the features with tempera or acrylic paint. When the paint is dry, spray with a clear acrylic sealer.

5. Cut out the shirt from the pattern. Turn the indicated edges under and glue to the front of the hanger. The bottom edge and the end of the sleeves will fold over the cardboard and glue to the back of the hanger.

6. Glue the face to the doorknob hanger, covering the top edge of the shirt. The face should be about 1½″ below the cutout circle.

7. Add buttons, bows, or other embellishments by gluing them to the clothing.

8. Using markers, write any desired message on the front of the hanger.

To add more color and allow for mistakes, write the words on construction paper and then glue to the front of the hanger.

Ages 3–5

Child can:

❑ Help to trace the outline of the hanger. Will need help in cutting it out because of the stiffness of the cardboard.

❑ Shape the face and make the balls and snakes for the features. May need help with some of the smaller pieces.

❑ Paint the features after the face is dry. Younger children may find it easier to use colored clay instead of paint.

❑ Select colors and fabrics for the clothing from a limited number of choices.

Ages 6–9

Child can:

❑ Cut out rectangle for the doorknob hanger. Adult will need to cut out the circular opening.

❑ Shape the face and make the features from the clay.

❑ Paint the face.

❑ Choose fabric for the clothing.

❑ Cut shirt from the pattern.

❑ Fold under the edges and glue to the front of the hanger. May need help with positioning.

❑ Glue on embellishments.

Ages 10–12

Child can:

❑ Cut out rectangle for the doorknob hanger. May need help in cutting out the circular opening.

❑ Shape the face and make the features from the clay.

❑ Paint the face.

❑ Choose fabric for the clothing.

❑ Cut the shirt from the pattern.

❑ Fold under the edges and glue to the front of the hanger. May need help with positioning.

❑ Glue on embellishments.

NOTE: Children in this age group will be able to complete much of this project on their own. They may prefer to create another design around messages such as "Keep Out" or "Studying."

Patterns

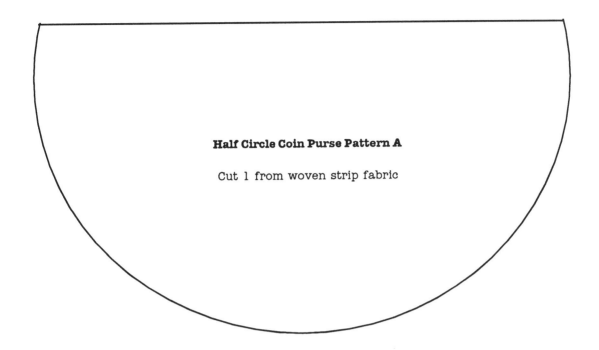

Half Circle Coin Purse Pattern A

Cut 1 from woven strip fabric

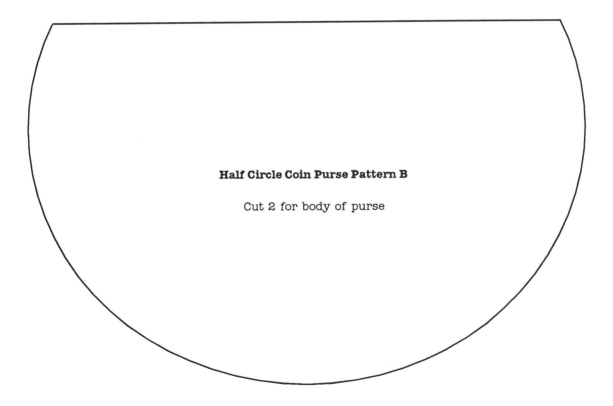

Half Circle Coin Purse Pattern B

Cut 2 for body of purse

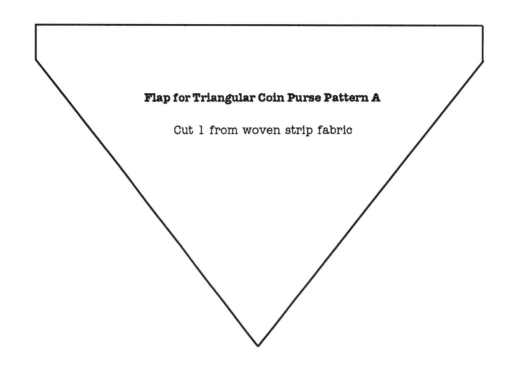

Flap for Triangular Coin Purse Pattern A

Cut 1 from woven strip fabric

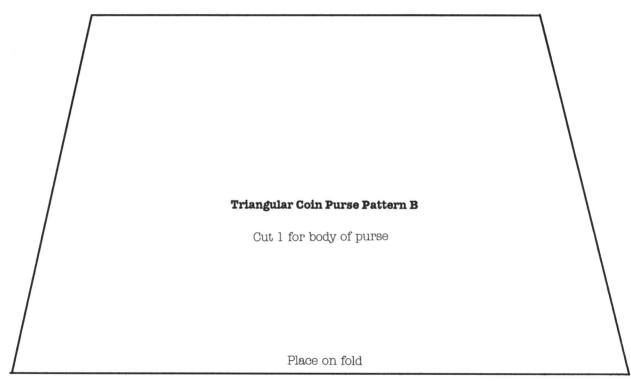

Triangular Coin Purse Pattern B

Cut 1 for body of purse

Place on fold

ABCDEF
GHIJKLM
NOPQR
STUVW
XYZ

Monograms

105

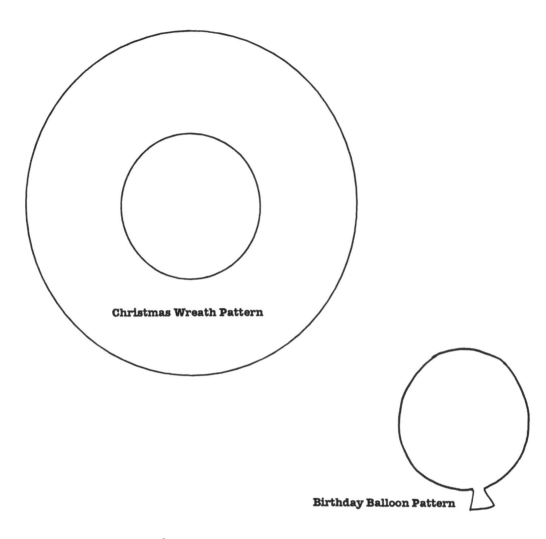

Christmas Wreath Pattern

Birthday Balloon Pattern

Star Patterns

Heart Patterns

Thank You Note Clown Pattern

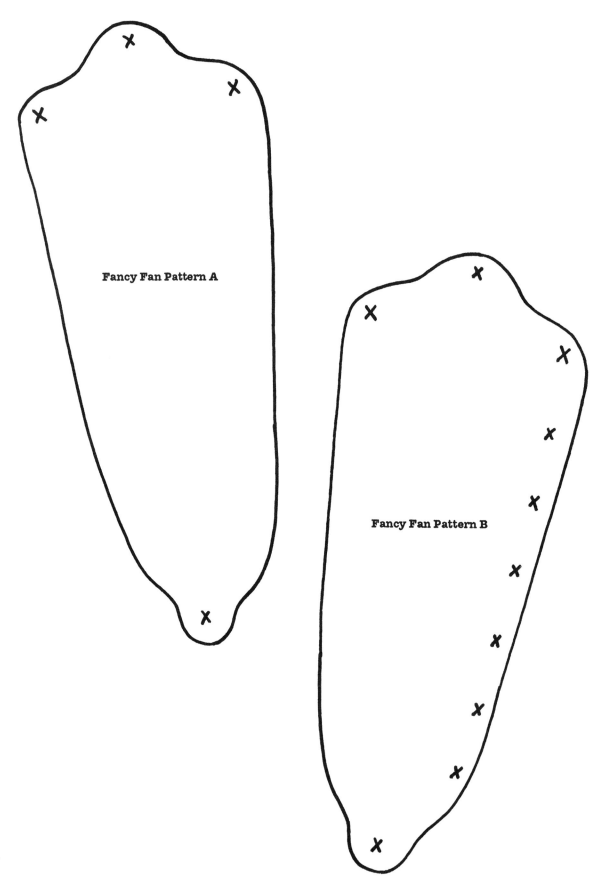

Fancy Fan Pattern A

Fancy Fan Pattern B

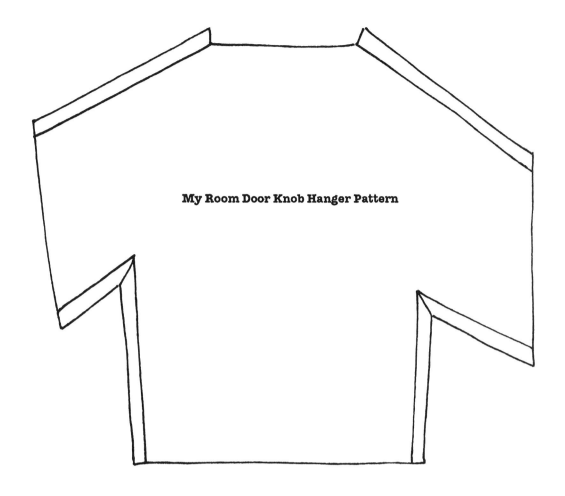

My Room Door Knob Hanger Pattern

Index